REEL ROADMAPS

TOOLS & LESSONS TO Become a successful video content creator

EDWARD GARCIA

To J, thank you for your love and understanding and for all the joy you have given me.

TABLE OF CONTENTS

ACKNOWLEDGEMENTS

I felt uneasy creating this guidebook since I do not consider myself a worthy writer whatsoever and content creation, specifically film, audio, and video production, is and will always be a team effort. No one in this industry works in a vacuum, and most would agree that the production process works best when teams can collaborate and ideate effectively.

Everything I've accomplished is due to a team of professional actors, videographers, camera operators, writers, editors, coordinators, wardrobe experts, make up persons, animators, VFX artists, audio designers, gaffers, technical directors, mixers, voice over artist, etc. They've placed me in a position to succeed. This manuscript pays tribute to those who recognize the power multimedia has, who appreciate how invigorating it is, and who have dedicated endless days to it.

The most special thanks belong to my clients for their unwavering support throughout the years. Words can't express how grateful I am to every client who believed in my abilities to create content. You have impacted my family and children for generations.

I am more than grateful.

BIO

A native of Queens, New York, Edward is the founder of *Dynamic Video Communications, LLC.* DVC is a digital media production company based in Orange County, California, providing end-to-end narrative solutions with a reputation for cinematic-style stories and unforgettable characters.

With a degree in Cinema-Television Production from USC, Edward has expanded his client base by implementing short-form video content that drives end-use behavior for global brands including California Resources Corporation, WaBa Grill, Miguel's Jr., Toshiba, IHOP, Lancôme, PepsiCo, JP Morgan Chase, Mars, Wells Fargo, El Pollo Loco, Taco Bell Corp., OCTA, UPS, Chipotle, Applebee's, Arvato, Advantage Solutions, LPL Financial, Long John Silvers, CABI, Del Taco Inc., The Pizza Factor, and several city and state municipalities.

Edward has received coveted industry awards, including the Telly Gold Award, The Communicator Award, ITVA Golden Angel Award, Cindy, Davey Award for Corporate Communications and American Corp. Awards for Multimedia Excellence. Boards Magazine listed Edward among the top five Corporate Multimedia Producers in Orange County and a recipient of the US Small Business Award for the best Hispanic Owned Marketing Business in CA.

In this new era of global, youth-minded multicultural communication, Edward understands the value of producing inspirational and relevant social media communications that can bring about change.

Edward reiterates to his team: *"Our mission is to be receptive to our customer's needs and react in a professional and timely manner - recognizing our customers and partners as our only assets for continued success."*

INTRODUCTION

We are living in a period of rapid change, one that presents us with bountiful opportunities to become a better version of ourselves through the art of storytelling.

In less than two years, the world has dramatically changed. We moved from a world where personal contact was the norm to a world where most people now connect and engage online.

Dressed in her leotard and ballet slippers, my 12-year-old daughter, Isabella, connected virtually with her dance teacher in our makeshift home dance studio. Practicing pliés and learning intricate footwork over Zoom wasn't ideal—but it became her "new normal"—it became our shared world.

Once Covid hit, and every business essentially became a direct-to-consumer brand, the importance of marketing and compelling storytelling became more important than ever. Businesses used to reach their customers face-to-face through trade shows, conferences, and office visits. Now? What was once done IRL has transitioned to be all online—and brands have roughly a few seconds to capture a prospect's attention and reel them in.

Now we are all forced to become exceptional storytellers.

Celine De Costa, a former contributor to Forbes, suggested that humanity is becoming the new premium. In an article written in 2019, she noted: *"When creating your marketing strategy, don't forget the bigger story: what makes you human?"* How do we accomplish this?

A simple approach is— through good old-fashioned storytelling.

Storytelling is essentially using a narrative to communicate a message, ideally, one that resonates or touches the right audience at the right time. When people are touched by a story, they follow it; they feel connected to the storyline. Brady's NFL journey with the Buccaneers is a triumphant example of a captivating narrative.

Here is the story:

The greatest quarterback is fired from the Patriots because of his age and declining skills. The 43-year-old lifted a moribund franchise, the Tampa Bay Buccaneers. Brady begins to galvanize his team with a winning mindset; he recruits former rivals and retirees to join his team; Tom Brady engineered the plan of action and is victorious – becoming an MVP and winning Super Bowl LIV. The game is considered the most exciting finishes in Super Bowl history. Down 28-3 in the 3rd quarter to the Atlanta Falcons, Brady stormed back to tie the game up and win the game in overtime.

All the while, his former team, where he spent 20 seasons, doesn't make it to the playoffs. This is classic movie material. The team's social media platforms exploded; the team's stock rose; Tom Brady extended his TB12 business globally; and hundreds of thousands of football enthusiasts became passionate Buccaneer fans.

A story well told will have prospective consumers buying into the brand. Therefore, storytelling really is a critical skill set in today's virtual world. Indeed, industry research has shown that a good 92% of consumers want advertising in story form, and this is where you come in.

Producing and directing short-form content is a unique skill set. Stories can build powerful connections with the audience because authentic stories build trust and transparency. Brand positioning using short-form, compelling video content is just one way businesses can break through the clutter and capture their target's attention—someone's heart— in just a handful of minutes.

There is a huge opportunity for video producers and directors to provide a service that is in demand. You play a role in making a company great. You can become a creative ambassador for a brand. Your role is to position brands in front of the right audiences, so they generate leads and become profitable, ultimately impacting shareholder equity.

The increasing demand for video production across various end-user industries, including broadcasting, small to medium businesses, and corporate giants, is expected to drive the consumption of video production, which is projected to increase at a steady rate between 2021 and 2026. Market conditions are ripe, and it is the ideal time to create, share, and make a seemingly good living from storytelling.

From early childhood, I have been surrounded by role models. My Aunt Fanny taught my sister and me for a while. My parents were teachers. The local police officer was a teacher. Even my clergy and coach in high school were teachers of some sort. It is a GIFT to have role models at every stage of life.

The purpose of this manuscript is to role model effective habits I found to be relevant to launch or build your business. The goal is to provide clarity and honest perception of the overall media (specifically short-form video) landscape. The objective is to coach, guide, and help entrepreneurs who are passionate about producing and directing video content to become successful and have a long, fruitful career. Some lessons are concrete and prescriptive, some a bit more philosophical to give you some context relatable to you.

It's time to put aside false assertions and insecurities. Now is the time to jump in feet first, build your business, and make a transformative change. There is nothing you can't achieve.

Sidenote:

Tom Brady retired on February 1st, 2022, after 22 NFL seasons and 7 Super Bowl rings. He exits with an unmatched legacy winning over the course of three different decades after rising from relative obscurity to become the greatest player in sports history.

Let's Go!

COLD SWEAT

Growing up, I suffered from a stutter that made me feel incredibly insecure. My middle school experience was tainted, riddled with major altercations with peers due to my stutter.

Often, kids are mean, and we cannot blame them for not accepting differences, and I wasn't an exception. I was simply an easy target. My stutter caused fights inside and outside of the classroom, in cafeterias, on school buses, and in the hallways.

I found myself diving deep into books, reading every chance I could, and reading aloud to improve my speech. When I wasn't reading, I was sketching, storyboarding, drawing everything from Shakespearean characters to Marvel superheroes. I drew from sunup to sundown, covering my bedroom walls from floor to ceiling.

Unbeknownst to me, the awkwardness accompanying my stutter paved the way to a lifetime of visual communications.

I remember one time in Mrs. Tina's class, we were offered the chance to give an oral presentation or recreate a book scene. The simpler option, of course, would have been to deliver a sloppy and unrehearsed two-minute class presentation, but I opted to create a miniature model from a scene in *Charlotte's Web* – just to mask my presentation.

I am fortunate to come from a family who cared about my stutter enough to send me to specialists. At first, they thought I had hearing issues, so they sent me for multiple tests. Next, they signed me up for speech therapy. While undergoing treatment, I realized that the only way I could communicate was to literally raise my hand.

My stuttering was not a medical condition; it was a mental limitation. I knew the only way I could fully condition myself out of my stutter was by putting myself in a situation where I was forced to speak. I needed to push through the mental stutter demons to move ahead.

Even at a young age, I felt that real change, transformative change occurs only when you decide to act. My decision to make something happen — simply by raising my hand in class was my first step to defeating my point of issue.

Decide first, commit next, and then resolve.

In class I sat hunched over on a gray wooden desk, my fingers scratching the surface of my thumb whenever the conversation shifted toward questions and answers. I decided to no longer be the kid hiding in the back row; rather, I sat in the first row, ready to confront my fears. Rather than avoiding eye contact, I hastily raised my hand when our instructor asked a question. My body was covered in a cold sweat, and I was immediately relieved when she missed my hand and called on another student.

The cycle repeated itself.

A question. My hand. Cold sweat.

A question. My hand. Cold sweat.

Finally, she called, *"Eddie, your answer…?"*

I remember it so well. I stuttered through the answer as my peers looked on. Oh my gosh…it was so embarrassing. All I wanted to do was to crawl under my desk. I experienced the same scenario over the next few months.

A question. My hand. Cold sweat. Stuttered through the answer.

A question. My hand. Cold sweat. Stuttered through the answer.

But the stutter diminished each time I committed to speaking in class and accepted being uncomfortable. Decide, commit, and resolve.

Over time, my stutter improved. I would raise my hand and be called upon. Even though I had a hard time getting the words out, the struggle nevertheless helped me tremendously.

My stutter is at times evident; however, what matters is that it does not limit my potential. Additionally, it enabled me to discover my deep love for drawing, writing, and creating storylines.

There's a lesson in this story – anyone can overcome anything.

Most people don't understand or realize how much control they have over their success in life. The truth is that greatness is a decision only YOU can make. You have the knowledge, the ability, and the courage to start something new. With the right mindset and unwavering discipline - nothing you desire will be impossible to achieve.

Striving for greatness in this type of business will be one of the most exciting, creative, and invigorating things you will ever do. You'll encounter naysayers and challenges, but don't pay them any attention – stay steadfast.

At the end of the day, you deserve to realize your dreams and aspirations.

By just skimming through this guidebook, you are taking a huge step in the right direction. My intention is very simple and intentional. I want to help you WIN. I want to see you push past what you think you can do, and you'll be amazed at what you will accomplish.

I want to help you develop the skills and strength to own your discipline in a way that makes your life more fulfilled, more connected, and more successful.

Decide, commit, and resolve.

THE HUSTLE POOL

Imagine two pools.

They look alike, but you don't know which one to jump into. *"Should I jump into pool number ONE or pool number TWO?"* I know is that pool number TWO requires me to wear a life jacket filled with weights and anchors. Pool ONE requires no such thing.

I jumped into pool ONE— it's warm and tranquil, and I'm easily treading water; I'm floating free.

When you look below, you notice bubbles floating around you stamped with REGRET, BLAME, FAILURE, SHORT-TERM STRUCTURE, DISILLUSIONMENT, FALSE AFFIRMATIONS, and I'M RIGHT – THEY'RE WRONG MINDSET.

I quickly climb out and prepare myself to jump into pool number TWO.

I dip my toe into the pool.

It's cold, and I'm unsure of what's beneath. I jump in regardless.

The weights are heavy and impact my buoyancy to stay afloat. This time, it's obvious treading water may be a bit more challenging.

Similar to the first pool, you notice bubbles around me...but this time – they are stamped with ENTREPRENEURSHIP; SACRIFICE; AUDACIOUSNESS; ACTION; STRUGGLE; OPTIMISM; COURAGE; PATIENCE; CONTENTMENT; and ACCOUNTABILITY.

You are in the Hustle Pool.

Everyone wants to get to a place, but very few are willing to sacrifice to get there. Pool Two requires a disproportionated work habit.

Do you want to be an entrepreneur? Know that it's a struggle. You are going to have to make sacrifices, accept dozens of rejections, and work tirelessly to make each day profitable. Because isn't that your goal – to be profitable while doing something you love to do? Are you ready?

Get used to being uncomfortable. Get used to the stress of the world trying to pull you down. Prepare yourself to have a moral and legal responsibility to sustain your company with real accountabilities. Prepare yourself to take on the responsibility of hiring and firing your employees. Prepare yourself to make tough decisions that will impact the very people you care about.

Remind yourself that adversity is the foundation of success. Being an entrepreneur is hard. You can't float – you'll have to constantly tread water. Becoming a freelance creative content producer is even harder.

However, life in creative production is an extraordinary decision, and there is nothing else like it.

Enjoy the journey and remember it's not enough to sit on the edge.

FOUNDATIONAL FACTORS - ONWARD

By no means is being a freelance producer/director an easy task. It's hard, challenging, unpredictable, time-consuming, frustrating, and scary. It reminds me of my father, who reluctantly supported my decision to major in film at The University of Southern California. Even though he was unfamiliar with the business of creating, he was aware of how difficult it would be. He was right - It's not an easy task.

I find myself having the same sentiment with my 12-year-old daughter, Isabella, who shows an affinity toward storytelling and media. The same pertains to Lily, my 19-year-old daughter currently attending NYU's Film Program. Making a living in this particular field can be considered difficult, and you must have a strong agency to press forward.

My dad always used to say *"adelante"* – onward.

Below I listed several fundamentals I believe are important to evaluate before taking the first step into producing, specifically for creating media for large bureaucratic corporations. These are critical to your success. They are foundational factors that will help you galvanize a career as you set out to build your video consulting business:
- Creative intuition
- Leadership

- High level of accountability
- Communication skills
- Team mindset
- Accept an environment of ambiguity and contradiction
- Risk-taking
- Perseverance
- Empathy
- Flexible, adaptable, and compromising mindset
- And of course, a Sense of Humor

Take these in. Do you have these attributes? You must have at least a majority of these and be able to apply your own unique personality to each project. My own eccentric and quirky playfulness have always helped me get through hundreds of troublesome situations. Producing has a lot to do with your personality in the chair. Don't forget this.

Additionally, you must embrace a simple mindset shift: It will take hard work and a good number of rejections before you can acquire clients and feel comfortable year after year.

I've written over 47 state and city proposals, some of which are lengthy 50 plus page documents filled with hours and hours in front of a laptop and a significant amount of money invested.

We were awarded 4 contracts. Four contracts out of 47 proposals in 12 years.

That's a pretty good ratio. However, that right there is a ton of hours spent researching, differentiating your company, writing, and designing; it's a lot of work. No matter how many rejections you get, you must keep going— learn from them and apply the lessons to the next submission. You learn to brush things off and press forward to fertilize your experience with every proposal. Sooner or later, you'll begin winning contracts.

In between crafting these proposals and producing content– What is your most important role?

The answer: Marketing.

Your role is to acquire new clients for your business. Your role is to be a marketer.

Marketing is the most crucial measure of success for freelancers and consultants in the media space. Whether you're a producer, project manager, director, gaffer, or whatever, your business will eventually fail without a constant stream of new business. In other words, your job responsibilities go beyond managing your existing clients.

Your number one priority is to market who you are and what you offer in terms of solving a specific issue for a brand.

MARKETING YOURSELF

My former supervisor, Connie Colao once said, *"Visibility is the key to your selling and marketing is a conversation about ambition."*

While it's important to improve at your craft— it's critical to market your skill set. Your main role is to be a marketeer. Your sole focus should be connecting your talent with an effective tactical marketing strategy to get you and your body of work noticed. Period!

When I started my business, I was making a mere 28K a year. It was only when I acted as a marketer that things started to progress. Do not be passive. Talent needs a cousin, and marketing will be your family. Everything you do—everything you touch should be looked at through a prism of marketing.

I've always wanted to write a children's book based on my daughter's ballet experience. *"I'm going to sit down in my office for a full day and put something on paper"* — that was my commitment one Saturday afternoon. *"The Ballet Journey"* was complete, and I discovered this tiny little story could be used as part of my marketing campaign.

Everything you do has marketing potential.

Be business savvy. Use digital media to share what you do and why you do it. Share your success principles. Share your challenges. Marketing should be a part of your strategic pillar to grow your business. Let your intentions be known, that you truly want to build a business and help shape the brands' communication effort. Simply mentioning that you are looking to grow your business can be sufficient to move a conversation.

Networking is a decent way to get the word out, but networking sometimes sounds too clinical and forced. One way to market yourself is to be helpful and kind in your day-to-day life. Treat every encounter as an opportunity to market your capabilities.

I'm from a family that's helpful to one another, for the most part, that is. They've helped me realize that supporting people is yet another way to market yourself indirectly.

A business associate and I helped our neighbor move out of their office during Covid-19 because they, like many others, had to close their business. Six months later, that same neighbor called me with a referral. She was gracious to introduce me to Diego, who became one of our clients. Diego recommended my service to AF Patrol. AF Patrol was interested in creating a video for their landing page. AF Patrol introduced me to Leslie, who worked for a non-profit interested in a fundraising video.

These connections and referrals were made just by being decent and helpful. Things happen for a reason, and this began with a friendly gesture to help one another.

What are you waiting for? Start your marketing strategies.

THE CARICATURE

"Care about only what is truly important" is what I mentioned to my daughter, Isabella, one evening during dinner right after sharing a story with her that I refer to as *"my caricature."* The lessons learned from this moment in my life have stuck with me for years, and my wife thought it would add value to the overall theme of this guidebook.

Here it is.

A couple of weeks before graduating from USC, I began looking for work— I couldn't wait to start my career as a filmmaker. My one-year stint working as an assistant editor for Chartoff Winkler Productions was coming to an end. The option of becoming a set PA wasn't what I desired, so I decided to take an active role looking for credible work.

I decided one way to stand out from the crowd was to replace the standard cookie-cutter resume with a caricature of myself. I thought, *"why not"* try something new. I commissioned a storyboard artist from 'SC to draw a caricature of myself as a producer.

Looking back, I wasn't sure what I was thinking. The illustration was meant to get the attention of production managers to hire me, an inexperienced producer, straight out of the USC film program.

The caricature version of Edward Garcia wore a perfectly tailored suit to demonstrate professionalism. A suit jacket, suspenders, slacks, polished shoes, etc.

In one of my hands, I held a brick cell phone. I was ready to connect to the world, well-equipped to solve production-related issues.

On my other hand, I held an open briefcase, displaying the contents, including "producer necessities" like a list of resources, a still camera, pens, talent releases, a laptop, business cards, a light meter, power cables, contracts, petty cash— all the things I assumed a producer would need.

Right below the drawing, my name and contact information with **"Producer for Hire"** were typed in big, bold letters, colorful lettering. It was awesome, I thought, as I had this twinkle of hope. My excitement was authentic and absolute since I took the extra effort to differentiate myself from other traditional applicants.

I faxed the one-sheet caricature, my so-called "resume," to over 100 LA production companies. During the late 80s, we didn't have email; the fastest way to get in touch with someone was via fax.

I waited anxiously for voice mails, thinking everyone would reach out to me. To my ultimate dismay, every night, I arrived home to a paperless fax machine. A couple of days later, a fax was waiting for me on my printer.

Finally, someone responded.

Someone took my caricature and faxed it back to me. This time, the illustration was a bit different— someone marked the caricature with their own biased humor.

My caricature wearing a suit was now replaced with a version of myself dressed in a Mexican poncho and a sombrero.

The hand that once held a brick cell phone now grasped a leaf rake.

The briefcase's contents were replaced with drug paraphilia.

The "artist" amplified my ears, noting "exceptional listening to hear immigration."

For some reason, they added glasses and a mustache. That was bizarre.

Finally, "Producer" was crossed out and replaced with "Mexican Drug Dealer."

I felt numb, and for some reason, I felt embarrassed that I took so much effort to receive this type of marginalization. It wasn't supposed to happen this way. I stood there in my condo's living room, dead quiet. I think my heart was broken. There is nothing worse than being treated differently or malevolently because of your background or the color of your skin.

It was one of those moments that will linger.

My associates at the time, Robert, George, Katherine, and Ken, really helped me get over the incident. I think they really empathized with me. But receiving the fax was only a moment in time, and it was time to put this behind me and keep moving ahead. Remember my dad's line: Adelante!

The experience taught me two things— when you make the calculus to be in this profession, you must accept people's frailties, and your role isn't to change minds; your role is to fall forward, persevere, and display a decent level of mettle, grit, and mental toughness.

When I stared at the caricature, I thought, *"what a waste of time this was."* The point is, we don't have the perspective of what's going to happen in the future. We don't know the outcome of a negative or a positive situation. We don't know if the caricature put a fire under me to work harder or smarter, of both. There are a lot of things at work that we may not understand. Bad things happen that may very well end up being great. Good things happen that can end up being tragic. We don't know. Some would say to allow fate to take its course in your life.

When you reflect on things, I hope you come to the realization that things aren't so bad and all the events that happen will eventually become worthwhile experiences.

So much of the success you'll have in life is really about the journey itself. It's not about whether you win or lose; it's about how hard you tried, moving on from obstacles and false perceptions, and nurturing the relationships you've developed. I believe those experiences and the way you conduct yourself will always be your scale of success.

"Care about only what is truly important and don't allow anyone to dissuade you from being the best you can be;" this is what my dad would say.

Sidenote:

Several days later someone by the name of Joe left a voice mail with the following message:

"Hello, my name is Joe; I just been made aware of an insensitive fax involving our employees. I wanted to apologize and let you know this type of behavior is unacceptable nor condoned. As a result, they are no longer members of our company. Good luck on all your endeavors."

EFFECTIVE COMMUNICATION

Communication isn't always easy.

Throughout my career as a corporate content creator, I've become acutely aware that communication is a multi-pronged entity that crosses over into everything we do. I believe communication is one solid way to build relationships and understand other people's points of view to ultimately work like a well-oiled machine.

Virtually every video or multimedia production engages or intersects with multiple communications channels— corporate communications departments, marketing, and PR agencies, independent writers, and editors. Communications is the glue that brings everything together in a successful branding, training, marketing, or digital media campaign.

While communications encompass a vast pool of professionals, the act of communicating must be carried out on a focused, personal, singular level.

Creative briefs, budget tracking, and production schedules help ensure that each individual stakeholder is on the same page—sharing the same expectations. On high-level productions, where we may have extremely busy department heads involved in the decision-making process, my emphasis on preparation, concise information tools, and timely updates are through continuous concise communications.

Regardless of whether you are an executive, a manager, a coach, a lawyer, a doctor, a politician, a salesperson, a diplomat, or Executive Producer of a production team, you are expected to be able to take charge, influence the situation, and make things better. Communication can clarify or obscure

This isn't always easy, and it can be especially stressful if you are fumbling for words or lacking in nuance in your communications. Being able to employ just the right words will help you motivate your team, inspire your client, and command.

I'm continually amazed when Mike Grams, COO of Taco Bell, makes a presentation without a prompter or notes to a large audience. It was a 13-minute-long presentation where he spoke clearly and emotionally without any stumbles or errors. It was inspiring. Clear communication and presentation skills are traits of successful executives.

Presentation Skills. Every C-Suite executive has this tool under their belt – it's second nature, and it's part of their daily routine. David Novak, John Martin, Marisa Thalberg, Julie Masino, Mark King, Greg Creed, David Novak, Peter Waller, Bernard Acoca, Javier Vasquez, Tanya Domier, Ron Woolsey, Chad Gretzema, Brian Niccol, Laurie Schalow, President Clinton, and Kobe Bryant are great communicators I've had the opportunity of working with. They continually inspire me.

On the flip side I've also witnessed a department manager who stumbled, stuttered, and had a miserable experience presenting. It was cringeworthy. Look at it this way— he was given the opportunity to communicate to his constituents and the brand leadership during a live broadcast. It was an opportunity to impress— an opportunity to showcase his leadership, and instead, he folded with nerves. I felt awful for him as he allowed the opportunity to shine fade away.

More than half of the errors and omissions I've made were linked to a lack of uniformity of thought and a lack of communication skills. Do not step into this production leadership role without the ability to communicate effectively.

The fact is no matter how successful you are, chances are your speaking skills could use some polishing and fine-tuning. Get moving.

LEAD FORWARD

The keys to success are PREPARATION, PEOPLE, PERFOR-MANCE, and PROFITABILITY.

Meticulous PREPPING.

Professional boxer, Anthony Joshua, reclaimed his three heavyweight titles by beating Andy Ruiz. He spent months training and working hard on the fundamentals of his sport. As a result, he came in 20 lb. lighter than his previous bout with Ruiz and with a specific game plan.

On the other hand, Ruiz came into the fight 22 lb. overweight. Andy lost a huge championship fight due to his failure to train and prepare. Andy lost his title along with millions of dollars of endorsement deals. The contrast between these two fighters makes for a useful lesson to evaluate.

Aspiring producers and directors take note. Preparation and hard work for every project are the most important aspects of your role. You can never be too prepared.

We had a shoot where a simple cable was missing from the video equipment package, and that seemingly trivial item impacted the first day's shooting schedule. Preparedness not only helps you, but it also creates the perception that you take your role seriously, and you appreciate every opportunity to perform and deliver for your clients.

As a leader, you must make sure each function has the tools for flawless execution. This mindset is especially critical in a live event. Is your IT person on the same page as you? Did you make sure there is clear and consistent communication between all key parties? Do you have a secondary system ready in case someone pulls out the ethernet cable? Who's responsible for securing the cables? Did you run a clean rehearsal? Did you test connectivity and upload speeds for bandwidth and outbound streams? Are multiple microphones available, and who is responsible for wrangling the mikes? These are critically important elements to the success of your broadcast program.

In terms of video, did you review the script breakdown with all parties? Are your permits up to date? Did you schedule food for the crew? Is there an extra camera available? When shooting food, is the fridge big enough to store assets? Does the food stylist understand their role? Are you familiar with the location – any windows, staircases, service elevators, ambiance, room size, etc?

Meticulous preparation is the key to your success.

PEOPLE

"Playing the guys that I thought were going to win the game," said Coach Vogel when he pulled Russell Westbrook from a game. This should be your approach. Surround yourself with people who will help you be the best you can be. Having someone below your standards of

excellence will undoubtedly compromise your abilities to create or win a game.

I can't say enough about the importance of motivating and preparing the right people to meet a certain project's timeline or initiative. One of my biggest motivators is a commitment to maintaining the highest possible standards to produce quality productions. This means picking the right person for each role.

Here are two key considerations when dealing with people: 1) assigning the RIGHT people and skill sets to the RIGHT tasks and 2) having a solution-minded team.

Your gaffer shouldn't be operating a camera, and your grip person should not be a DIT.

Every role is KEY— everyone is responsible for ensuring the success of every piece of content you create. Therefore, it's important to do your due diligence and hire the right people no matter who you are working for.

Your success is based on choosing wisely.

Hiring Johana to be the firm's CFO was one of the best decisions made. I no longer had to spend countless hours with payroll, EDD, and IRS tax compliance. She allowed me to allocate my efforts to do what I do best, creating content and marketing the business.

Equally important as choosing the right skill set and experience is choosing the right attitude. Making short content is a battle against time, climate, and money— you need a solution-minded approach.

Hire for attitude and disposition. Have zero tolerance for whiners, moaners, complainers, for those that don't show any effort, and for those who stifle creativity.

The talents' first touchpoint is make-up and hair. A makeup or a wardrobe can damage your production with the wrong attitude. Every person on your crew represents you and your company. Choose wisely.

As much as you plan and choose the right crew, things happen during production, and the only recourse will be your attitude.

Disney commissioned my services to produce a highlight reel for their Aulani resort in Hawaii. The camera package accidentally fell in the ocean during our excursion, including the lenses, batteries, and charger. Everything was soaked. We retrieved the camera but decided it wouldn't be prudent to use it.

Keola, the videographer, made a single call to have a second camera available that evening to continue shooting. Part of his preparedness was to have available resources. Keola's approach of what could go wrong miles from shore saved the whole day.

Another example occurred when I was producing a large opening video with a very demanding client. Not only did they have high expectations, but we were also a new vendor, and I'm sure they had their reservations. I knew it was going to be a challenging shoot.

I took the time to call each key member of the team and explain my expectations and the need to be extremely amicable with our new client. I put it to them this way: *"Imagine we are dealing with Tom's: Tom Hardy, Tom Cruise, Tom Brady, Tom Holland, and Tom Hanks."* That's all my team needed to know.

The two-day shoot went wonderfully, the client was pleased, and the agency recognized our efforts. They called us back to produce another segment.

Note, your job is to set expectations, set the tone, and hire the RIGHT people.

I recently shot in NYC, where hiring a small two-man crew is fairly expensive. John is an experienced operator, but I only hire him for one reason— his fearless attitude shooting in the Big Apple. I knew if I brought someone from my California team, they wouldn't be comfortable or accustomed to shooting in New York. John and his camera operator boarded his Segway and zoomed through Times Square to get the right shot, and they were remarkable.

Your role is to hire RIGHT to service the brand and maximize the content.

Lastly, there is a distinct difference between CAPABILITY and CAPACITY. Capability is possessing the background and maturational experience to accomplish a certain task. For example, a camera operator's entente is fairly uncomplicated. Stripped down, it's unloading the gear, set up the shot, and partner with the gaffer to adequately light the scene. In terms of capacity: will the camera operator have the ability to handle the protocol when the environment radically changes. Are you able to pivot and adjust within the framework of delivering the objective when an unplanned circumstance occurs? Will your background provide the inventory to make adjustments quickly? Your role as a producer is to provide the tools and tailoring habits to help your team execute the contingency and not allow the MOMENT to hijack the objective.

PERFORMANCE

Your objective is to create the best content, meet the objective, and ultimately be called back. However, if the experience of getting to your goal was terrible and uncomfortable, you will more than likely not be called back. It comes down to one thing, your disposition.

What do I mean by "PERFORMANCE"? If the client doesn't have an enjoyable experience during the process, if you are not adaptable or flexible, if you are not accommodating to the needs of the client, if you can't deal with ambiguity or the pressure of production, if you can't manage your team, or if you make poor decisions. It comes down to: How did you manage the day-to-day pressures of producing?

Did you make the right brand decisions during the process? Were you professional and adaptable to client changes and flexible with the timeline? Did you maintain your composure when knuckleheads passing by decided to honk their horns during your shoot? Were you adaptive to the surroundings? Did you exhibit patience? Did you positively interact with the executives or creative leaders? Were you a team player, pleasant, and fun to work with? Did you employ common sensibilities? Did you demonstrate a resilient work ethic? All these factors are important to your client, and they are tenable.

Usually, my clients are extremely busy, and I never want to be a burden. Instead, you want your client to perceive you as solution-minded and supportive.

Your goal is to make it easy on the client and make decisions that are brand-minded.

What are branded decisions?

I hired a producer to capture pick-up shots of a very busy drive-thru. Anthony wanted to impress me with his footage and was anxious to prove his capabilities.

We discovered that Anthony had to literally stop the drive-thru traffic for several minutes in the middle of the lunch rush to capture his vision. Not only were the customers upset, but the restaurant team was unhappy since closing the drive-thru impacted their restaurant's metrics.

Needless to say, he didn't make a positive branded decision. Your job is to execute without interrupting the company's operations, or in our case, the restaurant's profitability. This is part of your performance.

Brett, a producer for one of our clients, inquired why we couldn't make our day since we were scheduled to shoot an additional hour. I answered, *"…we felt if we continued shooting, it would have impacted the restaurant's lunch rush."* This is a positive branded decision because you are appealing to the brand's overall goal vs. your itinerary.

Because, at the end of the day, your content, whatever it is, is not bigger than the brand that's commissioned you.

Never lose sight of that.

"I'm holding your footage unless we get paid," one of my vendor partners in NYC sent via email. Note that I've worked with the vendor, Tony and Paul, on several productions, so this was a bit unexpected. The sum was a measly $1900. But he wasn't going to send the hard drive with the footage without payment.

Never run your business with this type of practice. In this case, we were working for a multimillion-dollar global company. Getting paid would never become an issue. Tony and Paul made a poor business decision. Not only that— they should have been exceedingly accommodating to me since they failed to bring the appropriate lenses. Their performance was immature and unnecessary, and unfortunately, they lost potential income since we would never hire them again.

I have a regular client that entrusts me with creating half a dozen mini documentaries each year, which require my cross-country travel to produce and direct. We have two meetings with the director of communications, the creative director, and the operations manager. One of these meetings is face-to-face, where submit a creative brief and a style guide.

I do not contact them for additional creative direction unless I have an issue. This is made possible by the level of trust and past performance we've built over several years. I trust them to provide the information and tools I need to produce a good piece, and they trust me to consistently deliver a quality product while always respecting their brand—with very little supervision.

"Ed, another incredible year of videos! Really high-impact great storytelling. I so appreciate your partnership and the amount of confidence I can have in what you produce without a lot of oversight. The videos always take the entire production to another level of professionalism," Bernard P.

We don't ask for funds upfront – we hire the right team, don't hold footage, and never become a burden.

Make it easy on your client.

PROFITABILITY

Is your business profitable? Are you adding value to your client's brand, product, or service? Are you making money? However, it's more than making money— profitability can also be viewed as being respected by your clients and peers.

Respect in the industry is being asked, *"Can you help solve our problem?*

Respect from your peers is being called and told, *"Hey Eddie; I want to work with you."*

Keep Preparation – People – Performance – and Profitability top of mind.

Footnote:

Anthony Joshua eventually lost his title of Heavy Champion of the World. He credits his inability to train and work hard. Working hard is difficult, he said. Anthony Joshua's size and punching power are natural talents. But these eventually fade. It's important to note— that more than anything— WORKING HARD is sustainable. No one can take that away from you.

THE FOUR AGREEMENTS

My sister, Martha, has always been an entrepreneur. In her early twenties, she opened a business selling water purifiers, and as soon as I left for USC, she took over my bedroom and filled it with her inventory. Today, she is a CPA, a real estate broker, and supports her community with an array of fundraising events. She is amazing.

My family members are filled with an entrepreneurial spirit. From my dad – who owned several restaurants in his native land – to my mom, who sold Avon. Of course, these business ventures were primarily due to income necessities, but they were commerce, nonetheless.

In addition to working for Avon, my mom was a seamstress. Mom had some crazy talent; she was continually commissioned to create wedding and confirmation dresses, create shirts for celebrities, and still made the time to create my film costumes.

Long after my parents passed, my sister sent me "The Four Agreements." She thought these tenets would help create the foundation of building a fruitful business.

They have always been important to me because they are so embedded in business success and the way you should conduct yourself.

Consider your own experience with the following:

Be Impeccable with Your Word

This is probably the most critical agreement but is often the most difficult one to adhere to. Being impeccable with your word involves taking responsibility for your actions. Your actions are the building blocks of your personal brand and your business.

Simply put, why should a client commission you if you cannot deliver on your promises? The easiest way to do this is to get into the habit of only saying what you mean and meaning only what you say. If in doubt, say nothing. Your entire team should adhere to this agreement.

Don't Take Anything Personally

Remember my caricature?

I have to say, it was only when I began 'SC's 310 class that I had the experience of being continually criticized for the work. It was meant to help you become a critical thinker and gain perspective. I recall an incident where the assignment was straightforward. Create a short narrative within 3 days using limited resources. After you screen your short to the class, you have the benefit of your peers to address their concerns. I recall a time when Tim, a fellow student at 'SC, was upset after his session. As a talented young filmmaker, he eloquently communicated the difficulty for anyone to be open to class assessments. Receiving notes and constructive feedback is never easy. USC's process worked, and it eventually helps you long-term as you progress in your career.

Know that there comes a time in your career when most of the content you produce will be evaluated and criticized. From the angles, lenses, lighting, grade, composition, wardrobe, to the editing, or microphone placement, your client will use their subjectivity to provide their thoughts, and they will expect you to make their notes.

I've reviewed client notes that are inconsistent with the ideals of the endeavor. This continues to drive me insane. This means you, the producer, will have to do some decoding to decipher ambiguity.

Remember, the content is about the brand, not about YOU. Comments and notes are usually made to improve the result or the objective. No one is trying to attack you or your preferences. It's not a reflection of you as a creative. Adhering to client notes is a part of your job and making their changes applicable to the goal is your commitment.

As a team, we must become less reactive and more detached from other people's thoughts; it's about the work. I've partnered with an agency owner, Matthew, on a couple of projects, and I am fortunate to work with someone with his patience and poise. No matter what the client throws at him, he handles it with grace. I've learned a lot from Matthew. Most of all, he doesn't allow himself to take things personally and continues to galvanize his client.

Oktay is yet another prime example of not taking things too personally. As an experienced DP, Oktay is a wonderful partner on set. He understands we are making branded content, not our personal passion projects.

I've partnered with editors who continue to debate client notes. Taking things personally can lead to personal importance. Personal importance is a state where we believe everything is about us, leading to us taking more things personally. In the end, you are left with a cycle of worrying about what other people think.

I've mentioned to my son, Julian, not to take things personally. Instead, I tell him to maintain a mindset that all their negative comments and actions are reflections of them. Often insults and unnecessary notes are tied to personal issues or an individual's beliefs. Alternatively, focus on elevating and consistently improving yourself.

Knowing deep down who you are, what your truth is, and that you're good enough allows you to stop seeking validation and acceptance.

Don't Make Assumptions

Assumptions often have very little basis and are only real in our imaginations.

Margaret mentioned her CEO's reaction before an upcoming video shoot, *"He is the most difficult executive you'll work with; he is a total and absolute jerk and will hate the production experience."* Margaret was 100% incorrect. The CEO was the total opposite; he was the consummate professional and generous with his time.

Often people will see their assumption as the truth, which is why assumptions can lead to negative consequences. To overcome this expectation, begin asking questions and maintaining clear communication with others. As stated, communication is the foundation for growth, and transparent communication prevents assumptions from taking hold.

This is why Ann is such a great partner. As a communication director for a large QSR - I've witnessed Ann communicate to my entire team without any false assumptions or ambiguity. With Ann, it's all about the details and explanatory discussions. Ann has never spoken disparagingly about anyone on the team. She is a phenomenal communicator and I've continued to absorb valuable lessons from Ann.

The simplest way to include this agreement in your life is to consider this: When someone or something surprises you, the failing isn't theirs; it's yours.

Out-of-control assumptions can often harm your production team and their demeanor. For example, I often tend to think my team can read my mind, and they end up assuming things. This is purely my mistake. I must consciously make myself aware that for my team to be successful, I have to make time to communicate effectively.

Always Do Your Best

Doing your best does not mean doing the best that is physically possible. It means doing the best that you can individually manage, which can vary by situation and your current circumstances. No matter your motivation, the essence of your producing and directing career will be based on always doing your best. It comes down to your character and your desire to become a brand's commodity. It's easy to pinpoint those who don't want to give their best.

Sue and Jason own a teleprompting business. I have never seen Jason walk onto a set without a smile and the enthusiasm to deliver his best. You can feel people's passion - it becomes contagious. Producer M. Wright continues to be one of our biggest advocates and never hesitates to help with contacts and endless wisdom. I consider Lori to be one of the smartest editors I've worked with. She's an intuitive editor with a wicked sense of humor. Our photographer, Steve S., makes the effort to travel and scout location to make sure he is ready to do his best.

Reliability is hard to come by. Catherine is someone I can always count on! I'm so grateful for the work she continues to create. It's rare to come across people who are so dedicated and trustworthy. Oktay and Leslie were in constant communication during the pandemic. We shared federal and state programs to help one another during Covid. We tried to support each other during trying times.

Along with a positive attitude, Dale, Omar, Wright, Nathan, Teresa, Alex, Andres, Jesse, Alex V., Brent, and Hunter, are great examples of selfless leaders committing to support their peers.

Apply these agreements, set your cleats, and do your best.

ROOM FOR IMPROVEMENT

Ken Chenault's article in Barron's stated: *"Be the person that puts you out of business."*

After years of production, I don't have any false modesty of how much I know. I know a lot. But I also know enough to know that there is room to improve.

Sometimes you must confront yourself and admit you need to make changes. By many accounts, I didn't always clearly convey what I wanted to accomplish. I seemed to struggle when projects were too layered and filled with complex communications. This meant I had to "fix" myself to grow my clientele.

The greatest gift you can give yourself is to help yourself first.

For aspiring directors and producers, it's important to continue improving and elevating the production process to get better at what you do. Think of it as updating your personal software.

During a live broadcast for Chipotle, I realized I needed to work on being more detail-focused. Preparation for live broadcasts is exceptionally detailed with plenty of moving parts; therefore, it was important for me to improve my capabilities.

We simply can't miss things—even though the client may not notice. I knew the importance of elevating my own talents and expectations not only to keep up with the industry standards but to satisfy my own expectations as a creator and communicator. Be honest with yourself, examine what you need to work on, and turn these liabilities into strengths.

To elevate our game, I've found StudioBinder, Musicbed, LinkedIn, Facebook, YouTube, Ted Talks, and Vimeo to be excellent communities to build upon. PremiumBeat.com contains excellent articles and filmmaker interviews highlighting equipment and industry insights. You can find a dozen of these to help you.

Hiring new videographers, colorists, and editors also provides production discernments that you never thought about. Music videos from top artists are always a proven ground to review and analyze.

Find your way to continually improve—be it music, network spots, streaming programming, feature films, etc. Finally, look for self-awareness and ask what's working? What's not? And why?

THE CREATIVE DIRECTOR

CDs can either be a detriment or value-added member to a production team. I've been blessed with working with a full mix of CDs with both agency and corporate backgrounds.

I was commissioned to work with Alcone, a local OC agency. The CD was fickle and lacked a certain level of mannerliness to his approach. He was more interested in the beer he was brewing at home rather than the projects at work. I was happy to be let go two weeks into the project.

I was continually at odds with Sue. Like every CD, Sue was extremely talented— but when you don't try to connect and engage in a meaningful way, you end up with a project that doesn't meet the team's expectations. In this case with Sue, we didn't have the same sense of creative acumen, and the existing corporate setting didn't help our relationship. At the end of the day, the client didn't appreciate our lack of camaraderie between Sue and I.

We were fortunate to meet Corrine on our recent shoot for CRC. Being the largest natural gas provider in California, CRC is a challenging client. Our CD, Corrine, was 100% professional and highly creative. She was cordial, amicable and knew what she wanted to achieve. She took the time to create aspirational boards to help strengthen our visual treatment and continued to refer to them during the process.

This is important; she fully understood the capabilities of our crew; she had the experience to know what we could achieve with our available personnel and schedule. This was extremely helpful. Our communication was concise, and we included her in every conversation with the client.

The fact that she had sores on her feet from standing on hot gravel for 16 hours straight was another sign of her dedication and self-sacrifice. The blistering conditions didn't deter her from getting the right shots. Corrine is a professional who cares and is committed to her client and the team.

What can you do to preserve and maintain a creative collaboration?

Communication is key. Do your best to set expectations with the CD. The goal is to do everything in your power to be an exceptional team member, and they will notice. Share as much information with the CD and be transparent. Have a conversation regarding what you think can help achieve their vision. Make a cohort effort to have a solid partnership and know that subjectivity is a moving target.

If these do not work, you'll have to embrace constructive confrontation. For a lot of people, this is hard. It is for me.

At the end of the day, the CD is a creative leader - treat them as if they were your client.

EMPATHY – SHARING - VULNERABILITY

One of the greatest joys in my occupation is meeting genuine, kind people who have great stories to share. The intent of several of our profile pieces is to get to the root of what makes an individual successful – finding the WHAT, HOW & WHY.

What makes a Taco Bell manager lead his team to become the highest-grossing restaurant in the system? What makes a Del Taco Franchisee so unique and so special she leads the organization with sales and transactions? What makes a team of young professionals create a nonprofit seeking to understand domestic violence? What motivates a 21-year-old to leave his dream university to create a fundraising effort to solve gun violence? What makes a mother dive deep into her career weeks after her child's death? What makes a daughter accept her mother's substance abuse to become an award-winning author? How an ex-convict become the best general manager for one of the largest fast-food chains on the planet?

I've sat with an award-winning franchise business consultant as she experienced an epiphany right in front of us. I was amazed as I literally noticed Barbara's eyes opening wide as she realized something that had been on her mind for years. It was an extraordinary experience to be a small part of this poignant moment.

These are my favorite short-form pieces because I've been commissioned to discover what makes them special. However, it requires work to capture the truth in just a few minutes of an interview. Know that most often, the interviewee will be uncomfortable and anxious. Put yourself in their shoes as they walk onto a set with lights, cameras, boom mikes – filled with strangers hurriedly making final adjustments – and at the same time, you expect them to be genuine and share their fears, aspirations, and joys.

Your role is to help them be brave, to get outside of their comfort zone, and have conversations of value, whether in their professional or personal life.

During the production process, understand that people want to be real, authentic, and transparent. You want to emit compassion and embody empathy when you are leading an interview. The interview process isn't necessarily a list of pre-determined questions and interviewee answers; it should be a two-way conversation where you share your story, and they share their accounts. I've discerned you must naturally be interested in people to genuinely engage. When they know you are listening, they usually reciprocate. This has served me well in many interviews.

The lesson is, to be honest and earnest with your approach. Let them know that you are being paid to make them look good, and your goal is to help them be brave. Being disingenuous will eventually lead to a conversation without emotion or trust.

I've witnessed producers try to achieve a level of comfort and end up with a basic question and answer instead of a deep, insightful, and heartwarming conversation.

There is often a point during the interview where you realize that the cameras and lights slowly fade into the background—and are out of the interviewee's sight and mind. And you realize that a real one-to-one conversation is happening.

I've had many instances where I wept tears along with the interviewee. You can't help being compassionate. You can't help hugging them after the interview. They are exposing themselves— becoming vulnerable because they trust you. You've established a bond.

Practicing empathy also occurs when the lights are wrapped, and you begin the editorial phase.

During a Del Taco shoot, we captured an interview with a general manager who dealt with personal issues that clearly shaped her. This time though, it was a difficult narrative. The process became emotional.

I knew we had a good story. I knew it would benefit the brand and meet my objective as a content creator. But I was unsure if we should share it. I thought that as sensitive as it was, her story and background might be too personal.

I chose to call the restaurant manager to make sure she would be comfortable opening up in a large meeting where 5,000 of her fellow associates would be present.

I spoke to my client and to the general manager. The general manager said, *"I trust your judgment."* Later, my client sent me a note that read, *"thank you for putting her first."*

Be cognizant that there are often consequences to messaging that reveal very personal and emotional aspects of people's lives. We must always be considerate of others, above and beyond the brand, and exercise professional judgment. When in doubt, always ask!

Footnote:

The Del Taco piece was a total success. I received the following email: *"Ed, thank you so much for taking the time to produce such a wonderful video. The entire experience was therapeutic. Because of your beautiful story, my family are taking the necessary first step in healing and restoring our relationships..."*

LESSONS IN FAILING

Despite obstacles and failure, you can bring about change.

While you never want to be let go from any project, there will be a time when a decision is made to dismiss you or your team from a specific project. And the feeling is terrible.

I don't consider myself very creative. And I surely don't have a particular visual acumen with graphics, typography, or humor. Be self-aware of your strengths and weaknesses as a director. There is nothing wrong with reconsidering the work if the skill set isn't part of your company's wheelhouse.

Several years ago, The County of San Bernardino requested my editorial team to move to another assignment. They were a significant client since San Bernardino is the largest County in California. They reassigned my team because we were not able to meet their unrealistic deadline.

On another occasion, my team couldn't meet the clients' expectations, and after several versions, Nicky very professionally decided to ask another editor to take over. *"Send me the project file and the footage; we'll take it from here,"* she requested.

Being let go is painful and so incredibly disheartening to you and your team— as it should be.

One of the largest online woman's clothing agencies asked me to send our footage back to another editor *"to see what he can do."* My editor, Andres, and I worked tirelessly on the cut— so when the email request came in *"...to see what he can do,"* it was a major disappointment.

It's ego bursting; you begin to doubt yourself and second guess every edit.

Know that experiences as these happen. At times, the client will have valid reasons to dismiss you. Other instances are out of your control. You may be asked to leave without any attribution. They can come up with a scholarship you may not agree with or justifiable. It's unfortunate, but it occurs. You can't make people behave how you want them to, and sometimes personalities clash. Creativity is ambiguous, and translations can be lost during the process.

How often do we look at the hard situations we find ourselves in, and accept them as our lot in life? How many dreams are lying dormant inside of us that are aching to be pursued? Don't allow a mindset of failure to creep into your psyche. It's a mindset trap.

What we can do is choose our ATTITUDE.

When released from a job or a particular project, we encounter emotional pain – because, deep down, we all want to create positive content. The key is to realize it's not what happens to you that matters; it's how you choose to respond.

We all have a choice; we can choose an inner dialogue of self-defeat and self-pity, or we can choose one of self-encouragement and self-motivation. It's a power we all have.

Yes...it's always about winning, but it's often you'll find success in losing. There are two parts to this lesson, however:

Part one.

Being let go at times isn't a reflection of you or your capabilities. But when it does occur, do everything you can to help the replacement editor, producer, and director be successful.

Do so even if they didn't ask for it. Share the project files. Share the selects, your notes, and your files so they don't have to spend hours and hours searching for the right images. Share final graphics, fonts, licensed music tracks, the grade, the XML, and any assets, and let them know that you are here to help the project be a success. Don't disappear, be an invisible supporter.

Be kind— accept your limitations and accept decisions with grace and poise. Even though you may not think it's fair or legible, be a professional and handle it with dignity.

Part two.

Don't be so hard on yourself. Don't concede to negativity. Be compassionate to yourself and your team. Don't be dismissive of your feelings of rejection. Be kind to yourself and try to feel less guilty. Being fired or dismissed from a project is not the end. Take it from me— it's not the first or the last time I fumble the ball.

In the end, keep PROGRESS as the key to learning. Keep trying to make self-improvements in every piece of content. Find a challenge in every activity and find energy with every project you accept. This is how you become a capable and skilled producer.

Sidenotes:

Andres and I continued the cut for the women's brand, and it was a HUGE hit!

Do not take abuse from any client. You deserve more. At the end of my contract with The County of San Bernardino, they ask to extend my contract for an additional 2 years. I professionally declined the offer.

WINNING LANGUAGE

Once released to the universe, our words cannot be taken back. Learn the concept of WOW—*watch our words*. Words have consequences, and words have power.

The words we speak reflect what is already in our hearts based on all the things we believe about ourselves. If we find ourselves speaking judgmental and disparaging things about our circumstances or those around us, we know the condition of our hearts needs to change. You can create a direct path to success by what you say and respond.

Practice careful, thoughtful, and deliberate positive communication. Ever since my children were very young, I emphasized, *"if you have nothing good to say, don't say it at all,"* and to this day, they rarely say negative things about people. It doesn't mean they don't provide constructive feedback, but they are careful with their word choices.

It's so easy to speak without thinking. Language is behavior. Incorporate the language of winning.

For instance, if you send an angry email to someone, you are the first to be affected by it, and the person you send it to will be affected by it second. But who will be next? Will it be that person's spouse or maybe their kids? What will that effect be? Is it worth it? If we all thought a little more about the third person, we would likely be more careful about how we treat others with words.

I used to work with Gregory, a talented videographer who sent me an angry text regarding an unpaid invoice. Be mindful of the way you choose to communicate. Gregory texted me with:

"Ed, I just sent you and Johana some emails. I don't know what's going on with my payment, but this needs to be fixed, NOW"

On the opposite side, this is a good example of being a professional from Alex V. when I inquired if he could lower this day rate:

"Well, I've been waiting to work with you, (LOL!) so let's do it. Very grateful to start a business relationship with you. Let me know what time works for you and your client on the 12th to listen in, and I'll send a meeting notice that can be used by all. Looking forward to it."

A bad example of how to respond when asked if Gregory is available to shoot:

"No, not available"

A good example of how to respond when asked if Jay is available to shoot:

"I'm not available, thanks for thinking of me, good luck on the shoot, let me know how I can help in the future"

Words matter. Words have a disposition and should be taken seriously.

Ask anyone who's been laid off – the first thing they may want to do is write a tempestuous email. When you are let go, it's naturally and uniquely ego-bursting, filled with uncertainty, and a bit scary. Your mind tends to wander when your next paycheck is coming, how to afford health care, or how you will be able to feed your kids. I never had those feeling when I was let go.

Instead, my *"now what"* turned into *"so what, now what?"* These words have power.

I've mentioned this to my boys Benj and Julian since the Alabama football program incorporated this mantra after their first loss. *"So What, Now What?"*

No matter what happens, you should stay focused, zero in on your goal, and don't give in to self-pity or frustration. Don't give in to the temptation to email or text disparaging remarks. Don't dwell on set-backs. Events themselves don't do anything to you, but your response to these events does. Everyone faces obstacles. Life happens – SO WHAT / NOW WHAT are you going to do about it?

When you use these words, they slowly become part of your vernacular, and you'll begin creating the language of a winner. When things get tough, and circumstances weaned, the words you choose will light a fire under you so you can keep fighting.

The words you choose will create new opportunities in life.

"IS THAT WHAT YOU'RE WEARING?"

"Is that what you are wearing?" questioned my wife as I was walked into the garage to head to a shoot. She continued with, *"That does not look professional."* Overly displeased, I slowly climbed the stairs and changed my wardrobe. While I might have thought my Timberlands looked awesome with my sweatpants – it pains me to agree that she was right.

Torrie Rosenzweig conducted a one-day course at USC for upcoming graduates to review the necessary steps for employment in the film and TV industry. She walked into the classroom and distinctively repeated *"Success is predicated on one single factor: Professionalism."*

Coach Jon Gruden reminded my crew that there is no room for off-colored jokes that may be misinterpreted. Even though YOU may feel comfortable with your client and the CLIENT feels comfortable with you - Professionalism needs to be the foundation of any conversation. Gruden would still be a coach for the LA Raiders if he added professionalism to his curriculum.

A production in itself is a unique environment – you and your crew have an instant familiarity. Most of the time, the team is up against an aggressive schedule. The crew, for the most part, enjoy their jobs. There is a level of conscientious task, filled with collaboration and teamwork. At times, it's very easy to lose sight of the crew's behavior and language.

Don't allow behavior as innocuous as it may seem to taint your decision to keep everyone in your team professional. I recall my videographer added his two cents to a conversation I thought was improper. I took Billy Bob aside and said, *"...we don't have control over our client's conversation, but we have control over what we choose to say and interject. Your duties is production, not to include yourself into a conversation."*

As a small company, demanding quality, and integrity from all your people is paramount, and there is no room for second chances or tolerance when it comes to an overt transgression that discredits the company in any way.

We employed a local audio engineer in Wyoming. During production, every other word this gentleman spoke were expletives. Even as he was placing a microphone on our talent, he continued to spew foul language. I had to let him go.

Jason was a local editor based in Orange County. After one of our long edit sessions – he grabbed dinner and returned intoxicated. I had to let him go.

Sal claimed to be an experience cam operator. I had to let him go midway through the shoot. He lied regarding his background and experience.

When Martin showed up an hour late, lying about his tardiness and putting me in an awful situation, I had to let him go.

Even when there is a final repercussion, compromising and violating the company tenets — the only recourse was to do what was morally right.

Take a moment to define who you are and how you want to be perceived. You are building a personal brand, and every member of your team has an opportunity to add to the perception you emanate.

I believe Torrie would agree: The foundation to your success is based on your professionalism. Your goal is to keep the following top of mind:

- Appearance
- Accountability
- Proper Demeanor
- Reliable
- Competent
- Communicator

- Poised
- Polished
- Ethical
- Punctual
- Decisive
- Integrity

I don't ever want to let people go since we work so hard to develop friendships and relationships with people we care about. Letting people go or knowing you will not be in frequent communication, if any at all, hurts. This especially hits hard as I know how difficult it is to land work and know that these individuals' livelihoods extend to their families. This especially hurts when it's something totally against my original initiative – to help people WIN. You must rearrange or displace your team when it jeopardizes your brand.

FEEDBACK IS A GIFT

Way back when I was fresh out of USC and working in a cubicle, Elizabeth was a Sr. Manager at the time. Elizabeth sat with me and gave me constructive feedback. I was immature and didn't understand the corporate setting. So, I didn't receive feedback very well.

I thought I knew it all. So aside from being deeply insecure and developing a sense of inadequacy, I wasn't prepared to take criticism.

Years later, a creative director kindly scheduled lunch with me and gave me very good feedback. I remember Lori was careful not to hurt my feelings. She helped me realize how important and valuable it is to accept and appreciate constructive criticism from your peers. I wouldn't have been able to be promoted without accepting help and applying the notes and recommendations from so many caring people.

A message to aspiring producers and directors: Accept feedback as a gift— especially from people you respect. They are giving you their unique and, at times, unforgiving perspective.

These people care for you and want to help you succeed. I feel I owe a debt of gratitude to Elizabeth, Nicky, Jeff, Rick, Connie, Lori, and everyone else who has helped me develop into the efficient and skilled producer I am today. Do I still have room to grow and improve? Absolutely. Everyone has ample room to grow and progress.

There are plenty of things I can do to become a better producer/ director: Spend more time reviewing other people's work for inspiration; venture out of my bubble and get uncomfortable trying new approaches; partner with a team to share and exchange ideas, techniques, and perspectives; work harder; work smarter, and explore growth opportunities.

Feedback is a gift. Be open, appreciative, and practice active listening.

ACCOUNTABILITY

A comedian once said, *"Broken promises don't bother me; I just wonder why they believed me in the first place."* But broken promises can be detrimental to both our personal and business lives.

No matter what business you're in, your success will be linked to your ability to deliver on the promise. It goes back to what we discussed earlier with the "Four Agreements" – your word is impeccable.

I recently had an experience where the mattress, pillow, and bed frame store, Casper, failed to deliver on their promise. The initial experience at the Mission Viejo Casper store was phenomenal. The location was clean, the sales staff were not overly pushy, and the product seemed well-engineered and fairly priced. So, I arranged to get rid of an old bed and anxiously awaited experiencing the promise of Casper's comfort. Unfortunately, they never received our order. And after getting the run-around from Jake at the delivery firm and their customer service folks, I decided to cancel the order.

No one was taking accountability, resulting in a lost sale and a vote of *"no confidence"* in the brand. I'm constantly reminding my associates that *"You must deliver as promised."*

Excuses and apologies aside, what counts is delivering the product. Casper simply failed to produce.

I used to partner with a talented and hardworking videographer, Martin. Martin was very, very good, with a positive personality and a decent lighting director. When you shoot as much as we do, we began building our own vernacular and becoming more efficient. It was refreshing to work with him. He was awesome and endearing. Martin had huge potential in our firm. Despite being passionate, and a team player, he lacked maturity, which eventually caused me a great deal of stress.

Martin had too many excuses. I recall his repeated *"MY BAD"* every time he missed a deadline or didn't show up on time. Excuse after excuse. In fact, I counseled him repeatedly since I knew he was an asset to the firm, and I enjoyed his company. Ultimately, after numerous mistakes, we had to let him go.

These types of decisions are hard to make— but know there is leverage when you choose to take accountability. There is freedom in your decision-making when you know you are accepting a level of responsibility. Accountability is your sword and delivering on every promise you made to the client is your calling card.

BEGIN WITH A SCRIPT

In addition to detailed creative briefs to guide a project, script development plays a vital role in the process of most video productions. A well-crafted script will set the foundation for capturing key messaging, giving all stakeholders a clear perception of the project, and will keep everything moving forward promptly.

A detailed script will help each department align goals and establish production requirements. The art director will provide visual support assets based on the script and shot list. The lighting director will manage expendables based on the script breakdown. The gaffer will know what type of grip is required. The colorist will have their palette. The VFX producer will have their assets.

You get the point.

I have supervised script development for a wide range of projects—from network spots and corporate events to training programs. Everything captured is based on the approved script. When the script is approved, you can freely work on the creative points, shot list, lenses, props, talent, and a rough schedule.

Scripts or a detailed outline will save you time, give you fewer headaches, and eventually save you money. Your script is your navigator.

LOYALTY

I recently had a conversation with my 23-year-old son about loyalty. Benj was working for PepsiCo at that time. He had an interview with a beverage company for a position he'd consider to be a promotion. Since he knew his limited experience would be an issue, he reached out to his supervisor and a fellow associate to ask if they would be willing to serve as references, should a recruiter reach out to them during the application process.

After about a week, the recruiter contacted my son and explained he wasn't offered the position because his references weren't very positive. Benj was somewhat taken aback since his Individual Development Plan at his current job was excellent. Plus, after his initial conversation, his supervisor said, *"I got your back."*

He learned an important lesson from this. He now understands that you will encounter people during your career who may be conflicted or simply not willing to help you, including people you are inclined to trust.

Throughout your career, you will meet people who are quick to put their priorities above yours. Perhaps Benj wasn't qualified, or it could have been something more insidious? Who knows?

Know that being kind is easy. Helping others WIN is easy. But it takes a considerable effort to be spiteful or malicious. It's a hard lesson to learn.

I have received a considerable number of calls during my career asking me about the character and professionalism of some of my associates. I have never given a negative evaluation. I believe our role as leaders is to help other people WIN. I believe you must bring people up, and it's our responsibility to bring out the best in others. You encourage them, you support them, you care for them. This is what leadership is.

That being said, I wouldn't be here without the support of numerous clients, mentors, and colleagues who graciously put aside their day-to-day priorities to make that extra effort to help me.

Loyalty is reciprocal.

Claudia is a training manager and one of our clients for several years. She asked if I would produce a series of training modules in multiple languages. It would be two weeks of shooting with a considerable amount of post-work. But there was a caveat.

They had no money for the remaining year and wanted to produce these immediately. Based on the brand's research, they knew they lacked training, which impacted their operations and, ultimately, their sales. They needed training modules right away.

I would have to wait 4 months to receive payment. I didn't hesitate to say, *"Absolutely, we can help."* We completed their training series in 7 weeks.

I'm loyal to this brand since they continually accommodate their calendar to my schedule. In the past, Claudia moved their scheduled shoot dates to fit my other obligations. She's been a client for years, and I would never jeopardize our professional relationship with a "NO."

The same applies to Nicky and her team; I'd produce anything for them (except for comedy – I'm terrible with humor). I've rescheduled my production calendar because I owe them my loyalty. They've been loyal for several years. They can easily pick up the phone and have dozens of production companies at their doors aching to work with the Live Mas' brand. Brett, Katy, and Andrew could call tomorrow, and I'd be ready to drop everything to produce for them. In some way, I believe loyalty drives me to produce great content.

At the end of the day, LOYALTY is somewhat trepidatious. I've lost what I thought were friendships because I believed loyalty was compromised. Throughout my years of production, I've mistaken friendship with business. Max, Jason, Rob, and Randy were all friends until the money and clients disappeared.

Be cautious. Loyalty is a balancing act and should be a strategic pillar to grow your business.

LEAD WITH GROWTH IN MIND

Saying NO is poison.

I'm proud that high levels of customer service and satisfaction have always been part of my track record. Even when my team is busy and low on bandwidth, I make every effort to accommodate my clients.

Turning away from work is always a very difficult decision. Saying *"no, we can't help you at this moment"* can undermine our clients' confidence as a brand partner. They reach out to you because they need your help. You owe it to them to be a part of their solution.

My first inclination is to say, *"YES, we'd love to help you."* But I understand that we may not always have the capacity to do everything internally. This is where my consultant background comes into play.

I've learned most creative professionals want to work with people passionate about doing great work. I've built and fostered a deep bench of talented freelancers to ensure we have the creative bandwidth we need to serve the pipeline efficiently and consistently.

The lesson is to never say NO.

Rachel was an associate manager at IHOP, tasked to create a short marketing piece for their restaurant managers. She reached out to me.

I don't want to say we took on the work reluctantly, but I recall we were on a major deadline for Applebee's, and it would have been easier to say NO.

Ten years later, Rachel grew her professional career to become a VP of communications for a large pharmaceutical company. Guess who she called when she required production? Rachel became a big advocate for DVC and introduced me to Chevron and CRC.

I'm grateful to have the clarity to know that every piece of content produced is significant. It's progress, and it's part of the evolution as a leader. Success is a series of steps and projects that may seem insignificant at the time, but when you look back, you realize it's part of your own narrative and distance traveled.

When you dismiss work, you turn away an opportunity to market your capabilities. Build your network of prominent and qualified vendors.

WORK LIKE YOU'RE BROKE

This is a mindset I frequently encourage my team to consider and adopt. As a reminder, I ask, *"What would you do if you didn't have an upcoming project?"*

You'd likely work a little harder.

You'd stay longer at the office.

You'd sleep less and lean into marketing.

For aspiring producers and directors— I urge you to take on the projects that may not pay your desired rate. Take advantage of slow times to meet new people, get exposure, and market your unique skills and capabilities. And when you do get these new gigs—regardless of pay rate—work hard as if you were earning 10 times the rate.

With any project comes an opportunity to find something that will excite you. Find something that will give you a glimmer of doing something cool and special. Every project has value. I was producing a piece for The Pizza Factory, and I gave myself the challenge to produce something authentic.

I've been partnering with Jesse, who takes on this mindset. Recently, I had him create a sound design for a new client that didn't have much of a post-production budget. Knowing it was a new client and the importance to me, Jesse didn't resort to the library of existing sounds. He knew he could do better, so he conducted a foley section just to get it right.

The same applies to Todd. His technical expertise, accompanied by his professionalism and calming demeanor, is what sets him apart from others. Our graphic designer, Brent, continues to create amazing and eye-catching visuals for any budget. Brent will do his best at any given moment. Steve B. delivers VFX content way above my expectations on every project for the past 8 years.

These are examples of what we all need to do, too. Make the extra effort to deliver quality work, and at the same time, build better, happier client relationships and keep the business lucrative.

LEADERSHIP CHALLENGES

As a producer and leader of a creative team, one of the less obvious challenges is to know when to be diplomatic and when to be firm on decisions. Everyone wants to work with passionate content creators who care about making every project reach its potential and help decipher the narrative and ultimately improve the content.

These expectations apply to VFX, makeup, gaffers, DP, editors, and set designers. There is no doubt that you want these people dedicated to their jobs and your team. Sometimes this means they challenge you to think differently; a different perspective and approach should always be welcome.

However, when pressed for time with multiple projects looming, I find myself saying, *"I'd like to try this, let's move on, we don't have time to debate."* You'll have instances where you can't partake in creative diplomacy.

For the past few years, we've been commissioned to create complicated green screen projects that take an enormous amount of time since they involve heavy VFX. Steve B. is one of the best in the industry, and when faced with challenges, he usually reacts with a *"There is no way, we can't do it."* But given a day or two, Steve will find the answer, and that solution will complement the request. The dude is amazing.

Sometimes a team member needs time to soak in the problem, sleep on it, and hopefully come up with a solution to rectify it. Give your team members time to digest.

Enterprise live broadcasting is relatively new to me. I've been blessed to work with a solid team guided by my technical director, Todd.

I've never met anyone like Todd, who is so professional with an incredibly positive demeanor; he's a huge asset. During the early live events, I was micro-managing the team; I needed to know each detail. After a couple of successful broadcasts, I learned one solid lesson. When you work with experienced professionals, the show will go on as scheduled no matter what happens.

A couple of lessons:

Get used to making tough decisions for the team and your client. You, of all people, know what the client is looking for – you know best, and that gives you the final say.

If a debate or disagreement continues, you'll have to make an even more difficult decision: Does this person have the right attitude to work collaboratively as a part of the team? If not, let them go.

As a producer, you must find a balanced approach and appreciate your team's passion and expertise. Recognize them for working hard. I recall distinctively when David Novak presented an award and recognized me for a job well done. It made me feel special and valued.

Lastly, at times, leadership is as simple as getting out of the way and allowing the professionals to do their job.

One other thing I'd be remiss not to cover.

Be self-aware that you don't cling to the notion that you are the only person who can do your job. There are plenty of talented directors and producers. At its essence, good leadership isn't about being indispensable; it is about helping others be prepared to run their own company or step into your shoes.

I've had the pleasure of partnering with Katy on several projects. Katy is a talented producer. When we work together, she carefully observes and takes visual notes; she's a sponge. She wants to learn, improve, and make an impact. Katy is developing to be a solid creative producer. Our mission at DVC is all about seeing the good in people and lifting people up.

Leadership is making decisions, teaching, mentoring, and coaching.

BRANDED CONTENT

I came across a good essay by Sven Herold, VP, Global, Shell TV, where he spoke about branded content.

Shell produced an amazing video that features the world's biggest turret. The video series shows the preparations for the world's biggest turret's sail from Dubai to South Korea for Shell's Prelude Floating Liquefied Natural Gas Facility.

The Prelude, Shell's floating facility, weighs hundreds of tons and stands as tall as the Statue of Liberty. I consider this branded content because it explores the people and the story behind this incredible vessel. Also of importance is what the content tells you about the Shell brand, how they interact with innovation and technology, and how they hire the brightest employees.

Branded content is often associated with entertainment content. The aim is to RESONATE with the consumer on an emotional level rather than focusing on the actual product. The end goal is to associate the brand with a positive emotion to create brand ambassadors.

Every time I pass by a Shell station, I think of the enormous anchors that took a specialized factory in Spain to create. Every time I see the

Shell logo, I think of the enormous task of bringing the Prelude to sea. I think of the brilliant minds, the hard work, and the planning it took.

What does that say about the Shell brand? What does it mean to you? Resonation can come from the most minor things, even a Crayola box. When my five-year-old daughter used to open a brand-new Crayola crayon box, the mere scent of a full, fresh box of crayons brought me back to my New York kindergarten days. The crayons were brand new, not broken in half with dull points. Oh no—these were pointed tips to virgin palettes of paper. It was a joy to start any project.

My mom used to make delicious Sunday dinners; her specialty was sancocho. For those without Colombian taste buds, sancocho is a common Colombian dish that usually takes all day to prepare.

I hadn't had sancocho since my mom passed away 20 years ago. I can't even begin to articulate how I felt the moment I walked into our home and was greeted with the surprise of the familial dish that my wife cooked for me after two decades without it. A flush of loving memories associated with sancocho reappeared.

I can't stop thinking of the amount of planning and execution it took the Taco Bell brand to organize a helicopter to lift their food truck and deliver food to Bethel, Alaska. Just from this effort alone, Taco Bell will always have a reputation as a caring brand— a brand that looks at ways to make an impact on communities near and far.

Most recently, I had the pleasure of watching the four-part video series for Houzz featuring Ashton Kutcher. Although we've all seen this type of transformation before, what stood out was the entertainment and emotional connection it made. Ashton's stepfather and family made this piece unforgettable. It not only entertained me, but it brought me back to an emotional level that will always connect to Houzz. In fact, I am using their online service to redo my home bathroom. Branded content? Absolutely.

This is branding done well. It's creative, likable, and it comes to fruition when we focus on happiness, warmth, pride, nostalgia, sadness, awe (Shell), or shock to resonate an emotional response.

No one likes being sold to.

It's a discomforting experience, so our challenge for content producers is to make the pieces entertaining with emotional value that outweighs the discomfort. Lincoln Auto, Dove, American Express, McDonald's, Apple, Chipotle, Google, Uber, NFL, Disney, Toshiba, and Taco Bell – they do content well.

How do they begin?

They begin by reframing the idea to relate the brand to their consumers.

Why does it matter to them? Why should they care? What clear lesson or message do you want the customer to take away? What value do you offer? What questions might the customer have? What advice can you provide?

Connections and stories can be found anywhere, as long we listen. We can find a story with a vessel large enough to anchor itself in the middle of the Mediterranean Sea or in a small purple crayon ready to illustrate dreams.

You must listen.

Your goal is to get to know the brand, their culture, their mission, and their values to offer ideas they can consider to be relevant, authentic, and engaging.

ADAPTABILITY — INTUITIVE PRODUCING

"I don't think things through enough, I feel them through…
I have to say, that's served me well."
- Francis Ford Coppola

As a video producer/director, you must be adaptable, ready to pivot at any given moment, and understand its relation to leadership.

I was commissioned to produce a brand profile for a large organization in Colorado; it was one of my largest and favorite clients, so I wanted to do a really good job. The budget was reasonable, and the client requested high production value—dramatic lighting, jib shots, dollies, etc. This piece was a huge deal, and they spared no expense.

Before shooting any profile – large or small budget— it's important I have a phone interview to get to know the organization I am commissioned to capture and tell the story about. Plus, it calms the nerves of some of the people I plan on interviewing. At this time, I share my vision and assure them we will produce a piece they will be proud of.

They invited me for dinner, and I graciously accepted. Dinner conversation revealed a unique story and an approach I thought would deliver their brand voice more engagingly.

One of the key functions of a producer is to discover not only the voice of your customer but the voice of who THEY ARE as an individual, the "real people" who are passionate and driven— the real people who drive the business. The dinner conversation was critical since it shaped the message, which I believe was important. I call this "Intuitive Producing."

I immediately called my DP and canceled all the peripherals – the jib, the gimbal, slider, dollies, and their operators – and ordered a Canon 7D still camera along with their Alexa camera package. I knew that my client wanted to engage the viewer with a Hollywood sizzle, and I, as a producer, wanted to engage in the most basic sense: human emotion.

No peripheral equipment can replace fundamental, basic emotions.

The next day, we chose to shoot each interview with a basic black sharp background, no music, with no video b-roll— just stills that I took with the Canon. My gut feeling was to capture the emotion without any "toys" that may distract from the story.

Usually, I never go against the client, but too often, as production leaders, we are hesitant to adapt and build on the emotional connection. The video profile turned out well branded and was also filled with genuine and authentic emotion.

The piece continues to be my favorite, and to my relief, the brand continues to showcase the video in their large gatherings as an example of brand stewardship. As a leader, you must trust your intuition and genuine sensibilities.

CONTENT VS TECHNOLOGY

When I was interviewed for BLURRED.com, they posed a question: How has innovation changed production, and how has it changed you? Of course, I answered with the usual:

"Innovation and technology have improved the workflow, changed the clients' expectations with higher standards, and allowed producers and directors to execute their vision like in no other way."

Production cameras and post-production have made a profound impact in the industry. At the same time, they've made everyone content providers – everyone from my 19-year-old shooting with her iPhone to wannabes shooting with a used Canon 5D. So, because of technology, the competition has become fierce. Now, we are no longer competing against our local video agency. We are now competing internationally, with our neighbors, and with straight out-of-school filmmakers.

I didn't get a chance to say that technology has helped us and changed how we work. However, the people— our clients— haven't changed.

People want to be moved, validated, cared for, and respected.

I recall the CEO of Taco Bell once said, *"People want to be understood, they want to be heard, and they want to be inspired."* It doesn't matter the technology or the platform through which you reach them – people are still people. It all comes down to content and telling a well-told story.

I had the pleasure of meeting Ron Meyer, Vice Chairman for NBC Universal, at a USC industry panel. He spoke of platforms, i.e., Netflix, Hulu, Tik Tok, Amazon, YouTube, etc. He mentioned that innovation and technology are only tools— some breakthrough— doing incredible things to improve the ability to reach more people. Still, none of them guarantee that we'll CONNECT with people, MOVE them, or AFFECT them. That's done through the message, vision, and content of what you deliver through that technology.

I watched Knorr's *Live for Flavor/Carmen* video and found it interesting how well the video connects with the viewer. It's a perfect sample of content that touches and affects how we not only view the Knorr brand but how they understand that content drives emotions. While technology will always continue to evolve, our human emotions and needs will not. It's the essence of every business— and its content.

GREATNESS IS ALL ABOUT THE LAST 5%

Several years ago, I walked into my home and noticed a small puddle of water under the Christmas tree. Immediately, I thought it was due to overwatering the Christmas tree. As I cleaned up the excess water, my heart sank as I noticed the floors began to warp. I looked around and saw that the entire first floor was damp. It was the dreaded slab leak.

The process of restoring the first floor wasn't as bad as the experiences I had heard from neighbors. That evening, the restoration company arrived and set up huge fans to begin the drying process. The 24/7 plumbers found the leak and re-routed the pipes, and our downstairs furniture was hauled away to an offsite temporary storage unit. We had to move out of our home for four weeks.

After the repairs and restoration were complete, we were welcomed home to brand new maple floors. Even though the restoration company performed the tasks expected of them, what stood out was their disregard for the finer details that would have made this a positive experience.

They replaced the furniture half-heartedly; lighting switches weren't functioning; paint spots were on the baseboards, and they moved in our large appliances without reconnecting them. I couldn't help but contrast this mediocre service with my production company's approach to client care.

We've shot hundreds of CEOs, presidents, and chairmen in their homes and offices, and we always take extra care to restore the environment to its pre-shoot conditions.

We take photos of the office before setting up lights and cameras. These C-suite offices are often exquisitely furnished, with numerous pieces of artwork, photos, awards, and certifications. By taking digital photos, we can ensure that furniture and décor items are returned to their original positions. Our team strives to leave no evidence that we were there.

Looking back at our recent floor restoration project, our service provider overlooked many details and opportunities to elevate their level of customer care and satisfaction. It was an unsettling experience having to vacate our home and see it turned upside down while repairs were being made.

On a positive note, the experience was a good reminder of the value of excellence in terms of client service, and it made me proud of the way my team conducts business at every stage of a project— because at the end of the day, "Greatness is all about the Last 5%."

INTEGRITY

When I was in my early teens, my parents taught me lessons in morality, courage, and patience that helped my approach to life—both personally and professionally. These seemingly simple lessons have cascaded to my children.

I grew up in Queens, New York. As New Yorkers, we predominantly traveled back and forth on trains. One day, as my mom and I were waiting in a fairly long line to purchase transit tokens, I tugged at her to warn her that we were about to miss the 7 train if we didn't get upstairs quickly. When I noticed the gate had been left open, I tugged at her once again and pointed out that there was no need to buy the tokens; we could just walk through the gate, head upstairs, and get on the train before anyone noticed. Leaving my mom behind, I rushed past the gate and headed upstairs, hoping to catch a free train ride. We missed that train because my mom insisted on doing the right thing and buying the tokens.

Right before attending USC, I was 19 years old and working in a New York travel agency. The agency offered me free travel to California with a first-class open ticket. My family and I knew free travel wasn't a part of the policy and bordered on being unethical. Even though we didn't have money to pay for a ticket, my father insisted on *"doing the right thing,"* so we chose not to accept the offer of free travel.

I don't mean to stand on a high horse, but as a small company, we have always tried to do what we felt was right. In other words, demanding quality, and integrity from all our vendor partners is paramount.

Recently, two of our partners violated that tenet and my only choice was to stop using their services. It pained me since they produced good work, needed the work, and integrated well into our unique team. We had to let them go.

We had repercussions, though; delays and learning curves, along with my inept communication skills, created a lot of work. However, it didn't matter.

In moments like that, you must look past the losses and be guided, again, by the simple rule that there's nothing more important than the quality and integrity of your people and your product. Everything depends on upholding that principle.

These life lessons made their way into my son's high school paper. He wrote on the topic of integrity and mentioned the easy opportunities to sneak into our local movie local theater after viewing one film and see another without paying, but was proud to say, *"dad always chose to pay for the tickets."*

Always do the right thing: It's something I continue to promote and lead by example.

While I partner with several editors, Catherine is one of my favorites. She is not the fastest editor, but she is the most experienced with storytelling, and I admire her integrity. I have never questioned her allotted hours, and I know I can trust her with any post work. Integrity should be the number one value on your list.

I still lean on my parents' lessons and advice when facing decisions. Since my children often come to the set, they see the value of doing things the right way and how that philosophy makes a positive difference on the end project. Even when *doing the right thing* has caused me to lose a client or a business associate, it's important to stand firm on your convictions.

KINDNESS

During my shoot in Milwaukee, my client, Brett A., literally stopped the car and presented a homeless man with gift certificates for no other reason than gesturing from the goodness of his heart. It was special since I believe kindness is one core value a producer/director should have.

Kindness is at the core, and how you choose to treat your clients and your staff will certainly impact your business. Be decent. Treat everyone with respect and fairness.

Follow this mindset, especially when mistakes happen. Be decent to people. Treat everyone with fairness and empathy. This doesn't mean that you lower your expectations or convey the message that mistakes don't matter. It means that you create an environment where people know you'll hear them out, that you're emotionally consistent and fair-minded, and that they'll be given second chances for honest mistakes.

I recently had a lapse in judgment and missed an opportunity to do the right thing.

We were on set and running late to our second location. On my way to Irvine, another vehicle accidentally hit my car. I stepped out of my car, incredibly annoyed. What was he doing? Was he texting? Eating? I wasn't necessarily irate, but I was rude and short.

The fellow who hit me was frightened, literally begging me not to report the incident to my insurance company. His voice was trembling as he realized I was probably more than likely going to report the damage to a Jaguar.

The next day, I evaluated the damage and reached out to him. I wanted to let him know that I would not pursue a claim, and I felt a need to apologize for how I had behaved immediately after the incident.

Some time ago, I was commissioned to produce a piece where we traveled all day and conducted interviews in a dozen locations. After the shoot, Nathan mentioned the media had failed, and we couldn't retrieve it. It was a full day of shooting, and I had to reach out to Chad and give him the bad news. I spoke to him, apologized, and offered to not only reshoot it but handle all the logistics.

Chad was the consummate professional. I know he was deeply disappointed and questioned our abilities— but he took it in stride. Chad is now a COO of Del Taco Inc. and continues to be one of my most trusted clients.

A great way of holding yourself accountable is always to embody and exemplify the values that make you a better, kinder human. Accidents happen. Kindness happens too.

When I began marketing my company, Greg Creed sent an email to his contact at Apple in hopes of making a connection for me. I thought that was cool. Greg showed kindness and has always been gracious with his time.

I contacted Liz E. through LinkedIn.

I met Liz a year several years ago during a shoot and asked if she could help me get a certain proposal in front of key personnel. I was surprised to learn that Liz had moved on to another company but was willing to help, nonetheless. *"I'll get you the name and contact info of the person you need to forward your proposal to,"* she said with no hesitation and no expectation for reciprocation.

I've partnered with a current Lowe's executive during shoots, but we have never had a chance to sit down and get to know each other. But, when I needed help, Marisa came through. I emailed her and asked if she could make an introduction to one of her colleagues with whom I wanted to pitch a project. Marisa, a person who is "crazy busy," quickly said *"of course,"* and soon replied with her contact's email address.

Even C-suite people can be kind and accommodating! Large, established franchisees have extended their hand to help. Brian Cox, Craig Langel, Dave Peterson, Lee Mitchell, Jesse James, and others exemplified true kindness.

I've sent hundreds of requests to various professionals across a diverse group of industries, and most of the time, I never hear back from them. For so many people, it's the standard operating procedure to simply click the delete button and move on without any regard to professional courtesy.

The lesson is to take a moment to thank all the people who helped you, those who continue to practice kindness and help you succeed even when there is no immediate benefit beyond the personal gratification of doing a good deed.

This is a philosophy and the type of common courtesy that I try to practice daily and encourage everyone to do so. Kindness is a blessing. No matter how educated, talented, rich, or cool you believe you are, how you treat people ultimately tells all.

PATIENCE & LAY-A-WAY

For as long as I can remember, all I wanted to do for a career was to work in film production. There was nothing else— *outside of boxing—* I wanted to pursue. Fortunately, I chose the wiser, less brutal path.

I grew up in New York City, where I attended Newtown High School in a small community called Elmhurst. The goal was to transfer from HS to USC. During my application process, I read an article on George Lucas. I thought, *""If George attended USC, Why Can't I?"*

I was admitted to the USC film program on a scholarship based on a small Super-8 film I directed, *Bat Out of Hell.*

Several years ago, during a 3-day shoot in New York City, I had this vivid flashback of a 17-year-old high school kid obsessed with acquiring a Minolta Super-8 camera…and imagining all the drama and action I could capture with it.

I recalled that the block around the intersection of 57th and Park Avenue was saturated with electronic stores. Speakers, cameras, receivers, playback units, lenses, cell phones, media cards, etc., were everywhere in the late 80s.

During my summer job at a Chinese restaurant, I would walk into the electronics store any time I had extra tip money and put down 5 to 10 dollars on that Minolta Super-8 camera I had on a Lay-A-Way plan.

It took months to pay off the camera, the tripod, lights, and film cartridges (yup, it was film, not digital)— but it took a generous amount of patience.

But once I had it, I took the #7-train home and started shooting a Bruce Lee-inspired film with the neighborhood kids as my talent. Our baseball bats were magically transformed into swords and lightsabers. These early martial arts and sci-fi endeavors would set the foundation for *Bat out of Hell* and eventually for becoming a USC Trojan.

Most of us do not like waiting, particularly if we are waiting for things to get better or something to change. Waiting is frustrating. Patience is your lotto ticket. Patience will give you the airtime to take a risk. Patience will bring amazing opportunities. Success isn't instantaneous— it takes time. I promise you, having patience puts you in a far better position to succeed.

MANAGING
A CREATIVE PROCESS

Managing a creative process starts with the understanding that it's not a science—everything is subjective, and there is often no right or wrong answer.

The passion it takes to create something is powerful, and most creators are understandably sensitive when their vision or execution is questioned. I try to keep this in mind whenever I engage with someone on the creative side of our business.

I recently hired a colorist, Alex, who is extremely professional at his craft and well versed in the art of grading. There is a certain degree of getting used to working with a new team member. There is a learning curve, new vernacular, and a trust that hasn't yet been established. The goal is to have your team members take ownership, do the best they can within the allotted schedule, and be open to change. So far Alex has integrated into the team nicely.

When asked to provide insights and offer critiques, I'm exceedingly mindful of how much the creators have poured themselves into their work. Make sure to communicate with empathy and understanding.

Instead of a text filled with strife or snarkiness *"...what the heck is this, it looks horrible... you not listening...?"*— it's important to perhaps change your approach instead to:

"Hello, looks good. Let me know if you have time on your calendar to chat. I'd like to discuss ways we can improve the grade – love to get your feedback if you have time. I look forward to your expertise. Thanks."

This simple, seemingly trite idea of respect goes a long way, and its absence is often very costly. The impossible can become real if you approach and engage people with respect and empathy.

DON'T ACCEPT MEDIOCRACY

If you want to perform at the highest level, you must prepare at the highest level. Mediocracy will damage your business economics.

It is unbelievable to meet production personnel who accept the usual *"IT'S FINE"* mentality. *"It's fine, it's only a cable spot"* - *"it's fine, it's only a training piece - it's fine the client won't notice"* - *"it's fine it's only a couple of frames."*

Whatever happened to the eagerness to perform better?

My camera operators understand their role is to not only capture the images — but capture them most dynamically. *"Get on your knees"* - *"Put on another lens"* – *"It's too boring, make it dynamic,"* I continually bark.

The same expectations apply to our editors. *"Cut!" "Let's watch it again" "Cut!" "Can we make this better?"* — Version after version, the video you are creating will get keep improving and getting better.

I've worked with editors who choose the first shot that works without glancing at the additional takes. I call them *"Lazy Cutters."* Don't accept zipping through the footage. As a producer and editor, the only way to solve editorial and narrative issues is to familiarize yourself with the existing footage. There is no other way— you'll have to sit down and sift through take-after-take.

Brands pay a good amount of money to see you perform— to see you produce. It's your job to be in shape. It's your job to be prepared. It's your job to review the brief— the script repeatedly. It's your job to be efficient and hopefully have the answers to multiple questions.

I'm often embarrassed to ask, *"Let's take a look at it again / let's shoot it again / how can we make it better?"* It's important to note that it's not about perfectionism at all costs. It's about creating an environment in which people refuse to accept mediocrity. It's about pushing back against the urge to say, *"it's good enough."*

Fortify yourself against the mindset of mediocracy — it does not set you apart from your competitors.

EAGLES

Fuel comes from the people you choose to work with. The people you choose to partner and spend time with are EAGLES.

As stated in the previous chapter, take time to hire the right people. Take time to hire a crew who possess a positive attitude and are passionate about their craft.

I've been fortunate to partner with people who care about our work as much as I do. Equally important, they supplement what I don't know. Alex and Andrily continue to educate me on grading fundamentals, lenses, and filters. EAGLES make time to coach and provide insight.

John Martin revolutionized the fast-food category, and I had the privilege to create content for his brand. During his tenure, I created content for Taco Bell and the CPK brand.

On my very first flight on the Taco Bell jet, we had an opportunity to chat one on one. He noticed how exhausted I was. This instance occurred during my early career, when I was shooting, editing, and writing – a one-man-band. John mentioned that it was admirable to see someone work so hard. However, from someone looking in, it doesn't show hard work— it displays the inability to manage time and the inability to lead a team.

John clearly said, *"…if you struggle with any facet in your career, hire someone to do the work for you, someone who specializes in a particular function; you are not expected to do everything, you are expected to lead."*

That was powerful.

There is a point in your career where you will lack the skill set to produce at the desired level. Eventually, you'll have to rely on a solid team to bring your client's vision to fruition. That means assembling a team of professionals.

I've been fortunate to partner with numerous EAGLES; Jesse, Nathan, Dave, Todd, Tom, Christopher, George, Ken, Lori, Robert, Catherine, Andres, Jose, Oktay, Leslie, Katy, Brett, Nicole, Andrew, Ann, Laurie, McMahon, Michael, Brent, Sam, Bernard, Stacy, Meghan, Sean, Steve, Paula, etc., just to name a few.

The team you choose to work with will help you succeed. By surrounding yourself with happy, inspirational, successful people, you feel better and are more inspired. When you act on that inspiration, you'll be more fulfilled. Fuel comes from the people you choose to work with, EAGLES!

At the onset of working with professional filmmakers, your role is to set them up for success.

I hired Nathan, a videographer, in 2014. Wedding videography was his main income, but he expressed the desire to move to bigger projects. We were tasked with highlighting a brand's new theater-type chair. Nathan was uncomfortable and second-guessed himself, which is not uncommon when working with a new producer. Additionally, to my amusement, Nathan couldn't delegate to my 15-year-old son, Benj, who was helping at the time.

Today, Nate is a full-fledged lighting director with a high level of confidence, allowing him to lead a small production team. I'm reminded of the time at the Ontario Airport when the director of operations asked Nate if he needed something— Nate responded, *"Can you move the 747 Boeing to place it in the best light?"* They moved the plane for us. Nathan has moved on to bigger things and we are extremely proud of his endeavors.

During a live broadcast, every member of your team is critical, especially the audio engineer, who is a key member of the team. I met our audio engineer through a recommendation, and Dave has turned out to be a total EAGLE.

There is nothing like having a team member who showcases his commitment to me and the project's objective. Dave is fully committed to the success of each of our projects. His willingness to step up and do what needs to be done is awesome — even if it falls outside of his job description. His value did not go unnoticed when he took the initiative to find his replacement, train him, and follow up on his successor.

Years ago, on a Sunday morning, Andres walked into my office, fingers shaking, voice stuttering, and my uncertainty filled the edit room. It was his first time working with me as an editor. Six years later, Andres has become a trusted and proficient editor. It's wonderful to see his growth as an editor and human being. We've had challenges, but I see something in Andres, the ability to keep growing above his potential.

Roberto R. knocked on my condo door 15 years ago and said: *"Sir, your car is leaking oil."* From that point, Roberto began his film and video production career. There was once a time when he was on every production. He even had a small part in our first feature film. With every shooting experience, Roberto became more and more comfortable. He learned to speak English, gained confidence, and saved a considerable amount of money to open his own thriving business. Even though we don't work together as much, he is one of my most trusted confidants. Roberto is an EAGLE with his own flourishing company.

Value ABILITY more than experience and put people in roles that require more of them than they know they have within., which is exactly what we did for Roberto, Nathan, Andres, and countless others.

We help people WIN.

The bottom line is that achieving your video production objectives requires much more than solely camera operators and editors. Exemplary content is produced by a slew of talented and passionate storytellers who are ready to be coached, who exercise process and discipline while adhering to your expectations.

ABSOLUTELY

As a freelance producer, one of your goals is to create consistency in your work. You create consistency by providing unparalleled service to each client. That means not only exceeding the expectations but being responsive, available, and flexible.

Your first and most important question to your client should be, *"how may I help you meet your business goals?"* Starting a new relationship this way displays an eagerness to do great work.

Too often, less experienced producers and directors are focused on trivial issues and policies, such as insisting on being paid the day of the shoot, scheduling lunch as a priority, the reluctance with an early crew call, the unwillingness to meet a project deadline, etc.

When clients encounter those types of "speed bumps," they tend to move on to another company. The goal of a producer is always to be part of the solution and make the process easier, not complicate it.

Be of service to your client. Make it easy on them.

My clients are usually extremely busy people. They have deadlines, stress, and pressure that we may not understand. It's important to help, even if it's not directly associated with your role.

We book hotels for the clientele if it makes it easier. We coordinate the travel. We plan meals. We ensure that our client has WIFI access before their arrival. And we make sure the location has ample vehicle space. I was more than willing to move my crews' vehicles to make room for my client. Doing these things creates a kinship with your client and allows them to really focus on the task at hand.

At every step, you must meet and aim to exceed the clients' expectations.

We had a gaffer who decided to take a break and have breakfast while his DP continued to work and set up lights. We were under pressure to get the company to move to the next location, and the gaffer continued to eat. He had a right to take lunch. However, he lacked sensibilities. Every member of the crew must always be of service within their capacity or outside their role— even if it breaks standard policies, such as a meal break.

We had a large shoot with multiple executives in attendance and it was an aggressive schedule. During the day, the CEO asked if he could be moved his segment earlier, meaning we had to configure the entire day to fit the CEO's schedule. My DP, Oktay, said without hesitation: ABSOLUTELY.

During the last 8 minutes of a live broadcast, where we were streaming to over 45K viewers, the client asked me if we had the capability to update the presenter's PowerPoint. *"It would be awesome to update them and be as current as possible"* said Ann. Todd, our technical director, had one thing to say: ABSOLUTELY. With less than 2 minutes before going live, we updated the content.

We were booked for a half day to capture Tanya Domier. She was 3 hours late owning to the fact she was finalizing the details with Walmart. We were asked if we would extend the day: ABSOLUTELY.

Your team should never complain. Your team should be able to have the know-how and experience to make things happen. A client does not appreciate a video production crew complaining or making a fuss.

Your job as a leader is to be a solution funnel. And this consistency is marketable to attract new clients.

Do your job well and be patient. Seek opportunities to pitch in and expand and to become one of the people who your bosses know they can turn to when an opportunity arises.

FINANCIAL STRENGTH

We're not making a feature film or a network Super Bowl spot, and we are not producing the Grammys.

What we are most likely producing is short-form video content, running somewhere between 5-200K.

The last thing you want to do is ask your client for money upfront for production less than 50K. I understand you may have different scenarios; however, having available funds in your company is a sign that you are a successful, well-managed, anticipatory organization.

I will never forget the conversation I had with a new client when I was building my company.

A client for a sandwich brand mentioned, *"...if you can't afford to put your small team in a hotel for the duration of the shoot, you shouldn't be supporting such a large brand like ours."* When I asked if he was willing to use his company credit card to absorb the hotel cost, that was his response. His response can be interpreted as being rude, but he was correct.

Most recently, a Milwaukee production firm was adamant regarding their 2000.00 invoice. The mail was slow, and the check was delayed due to the holidays. They sent me an email, text, and left voicemails with *"…we haven't received the check, and we can't pay our people."* It was appa-rent the agency was too small or not well-managed. Two thousand dollars shouldn't be an issue. You must be able to float your company and not be burdened to your client. Reminder – your client's goal is to solve an issue— do not be a burden to them— this is part of your performance.

Sidenote:

Establish a credit line with your local bank or credit union.

PRODUCTION INSURANCE

Get production insurance.

There is nothing more important than acquiring insurance for your company and team. I partner with a small video wedding company that doesn't carry insurance. The owner is under the impression that his LLC will take the brunt of the burden or the hardship if something happens.

He is mistaken.

Do not fall into the LLC misinformation.

Your LLC will not be able to fully protect you if something happens to your gear, team, or facility. It is irresponsible not to carry protection. Additionally, large brands will require insurance status with a certificate of insurance. Insurance is another level of professionalism your client will expect you to have.

DATA IS KING

In today's digital age, information/data truly is "king."

The success of the world's most powerful companies — Google, Amazon, Apple, Facebook, etc.— are driven by information science, along with the responsibility to safeguard sensitive data.

Gathering data is the first step in creating engagement. The more we know about the audiences and personas we're trying to influence, the greater our chances of success. In our industry, information management includes tapping into databases to identify key performance indicators or KPIs.

I collect KPIs from my large global clients—Chevron, Logitech, and CRC. The information gathered helps my team develop strategies that will benefit the client in multiple areas.

When creating video communications without leveraging data, you are merely hoping for the best. These days we can research and track a myriad of metrics that give us insight into the minds of our intended audiences.

But you also have to recognize that there is never 100% certainty. No matter how much data you've been given, it's still, ultimately, a risk, and the decision to take that risk or not comes down to one person's instinct. More on intuitive producing.

TRUST & VERIFY

Small mistakes and errors are nearly always preventable, but they can be costly and embarrassing.

Several years ago, we submitted what we believed to be a final graded and mixed asset to my client. During their rehearsals, the client caught a title error that should never have been approved. It was so blatant, infuriating, and unprofessional that I'm still kicking myself.

These things should never happen regardless of how busy you are.

Lessons learned— Always take the time to sit down, focus, and review each piece prior to deliverables. It's not a matter of trusting or relying on someone else…it's really about ownership and verification. It's an obligation to your client and your business; it's your reputation that's on the line, which can have an impact on your future revenues.

I request my editors do a quality check for every piece before client delivery. Even then, I've found errors and dumb mistakes. It used to make my blood boil. Then my CFO mentioned it would be unrealistic to have these expectations of your team, and as a leader, it's your company, and you are the embodiment of that company.

What that means is this: Your values— your sense of integrity and decency and honesty, the way you comport yourself in the world—are a stand-in for the company's values. If there is a message you should take away, remember it's your company.

You can be the head of a seventy-person or seven-person organization or a single member— no one is going to care as much as you will.

FOCUS ON YOUR HEALTH
AND WELL-BEING

He was a zombie from the Walking Dead.

Bakersfield, California. It was 105 degrees in the middle of this long production day. We made provisions to have plenty of water for talent and crew easily available. We hired a PA to oversee our water supply during the day. Our trusted photographer, Steve S., was so immersed in getting the right shots that he forgot to hydrate.

Steve looked terrible and suffering from a lack of water. Bless his heart for his passion but looked like a zombie.

In the fast-paced world of video shoots and production, it can be very challenging for video crews to eat healthily and exercise good nutritional habits on the job.

Quite often, there isn't enough time to sit down, relax, and consume a healthy meal. This is awful since I strongly believe that we'll have more energy and a better mindset for performing our specialized and technical tasks if we take care of our bodies.

According to the National Institutes of Health, aerobic exercise and other forms of movement are linked to reducing depression, stress, and anxiety. Getting your body moving and engaging in exercise comes with a series of other health benefits. This means that your emotional and physical health can impact your mental health and vice versa. For these reasons, getting regular exercise can only help you.

I jokingly use the term – *"Put the donut down."* Putting the donut down means embracing discipline; being a better version of yourself, leading a healthier lifestyle, and avoiding the donut shop that lurks on every corner.

Exercising comes down to one thing: Discipline. Discipline to act. It doesn't take much. Even light stretching, jogging in a park, or running for ten minutes on a treadmill a few times per week can work wonders.

I've been exercising since high school, and I realize that it's DISCI-PLINE that takes me to the gym at 5 am. It's the same discipline I apply in the production world; the discipline it takes to review one more piece of music, the discipline to review a cut one more time. Discipline helps you bring on positive productive habits.

Let me be honest, I'm pathetic – I run 5.2 miles in 47 minutes. A total loser runner. Nonetheless, I notice my stress level is reduced significantly every day I spend time in the gym.

Exercise and reducing stress can only positively improve the quality of your life and your production business. It can also improve your interpersonal relationships, manner of processing information, and ability to deal with challenges. Each of these factors impacts your ability to move through the world and productively carry yourself. Exercise helps in many ways, but the reduction of stress most certainly takes the cake.

My editors will attest to the fact that I can fall asleep anywhere. Because regular exercise increases the physical temperature of your body, your brain can have an easier time winding down to sleep at night or taking power naps.

As you can imagine, all of this can impact the quality of your mental health and how you see the world.

Weight Training.

Yoga.

Walking.

Palates.

Anything to keep you moving. Find your strength.

COMPETITIVE SPIRIT

People often think that being competitive is negative.

They think being competitive means finger-pointing, backstabbing, demeaning remarks, disparaging comments, and thieves who steal your ideas and grab your glory.

I define being competitive in the production arena as having a competitive spirit that will leverage you to grow and position you for future success. I believe what makes a great entrepreneur is their competitiveness to be great. And it's something I encourage everyone to embrace.

Embrace the grind. Embrace the work. Realizing your potential and making progress is what I believe to be the essence of your competitive spirit.

Stay with it.

GRATITUDE, HUMILITY & BLESSINGS

My dad was a ferocious reader...a very astute observer...a gracious man with ambition and clarity. He was also an immigrant, a Hispanic who left his homeland to travel to NYC to find a better life.

New York is a tough town, and I can only imagine how difficult it was for both my parents to step into this world without the gravity of language. For those unacquainted with the Big Apple, there is a certain way New Yorkers communicate. Assimilating into the life of a non-native New Yorker must have been hard.

My dad passed away when he was 93, and I've always felt he never had the type of opportunity to live up to the potential he really had. I've always felt he believed his life didn't amount to much, except for his children.

Before the onset of his dementia, it was extraordinary to feel his enthusiasm and endless unconditional support in every conversation we shared. In his eyes, even the simplest pieces I created were "amazing," and the behind-the-scenes pictures I sent were viewed as if I were producing **The Godfather** or **The Empire Strikes Back**. It was always *"you can do it; work hard; nothing can stop you; you are blessed and favored."*

It's only now that I'm beginning to realize what a profound influence, he had allowing me to follow my dreams—which has made me deeply emotional. At the core of my story are my parents. My dad kept his sights on what was truly important. My parents were filled with gratitude. My father practiced humility no matter the circumstance he was placed in, and ultimately, he was a man of faith.

Gratitude is the strongest and most influential trait to be successful in any business you choose to undertake. Saying *"thank you"* means that we recognize the gifts that come into our lives and, as a result, acknowledge the value of other people. Very simply, gratitude can make us less self-focused and more focused on those around us—a hallmark of humble people.

I also believe you must approach production and life with a sense of genuine humility. The success you will enjoy will be due in part to your efforts and hard work, but it's also been due to so much beyond yourself, the actions and support of so many people, and to the unexpected blessings and prayers.

RECOGNITION

Recognition is currency.

One of the things I learned during my YUM! tenure was the power of recognition. David Novak built a culture of recognition during his tenure as CEO. It was awesome and special to witness a positive shift in the brands' culture. He made it permissible for all of us to lead by his example.

Recognition is about motivating and encouraging your team to do their best and go beyond their capabilities.

I've had experiences where my recognition efforts developed into coaching, mentoring, and building personal connections. The power of appreciation is huge, and you must make this a part of your creative organization. Especially in content creation where usually your team will put their hearts and souls into every project.

"Thanks for being punctual"

"Thank you for being so professional"

"Thank you for taking the extra time to clean up after your work"

"Thanks for taking time to learn a new program"

I believe there is magic in recognition.

When you address someone's strength, it shows that you care; it tells them you see them and appreciate their efforts.

There is always an opportunity to recognize someone's work or punctuality or attitude or growth, anything. There is always a time to tell someone how you appreciate them— the gaffer who works nonstop, the grip who volunteers to help, the make-up lady who cleanses the talent after they are done, the DP who sets up a courtesy, the wardrobe who stands-in for the talent, or the PA that hustled throughout the day. We have moments where you can make time to appreciate someone else's efforts. The same applies to your client. There is no reason why you can't recognize your clients.

"Thank you for helping my small business grow" is how I usually end my conversation with our clients.

Remember to take the time to recognize how others contribute to your own success.

My father taught me the importance of building trust by expressing gratitude and staying humble, and I encourage you to follow his path too.

I urge you to try it – it may work wonders for you professionally and personally.

CONCLUSION: DISCIPLINE

A word that gets used in leadership is *discipline*. I left this specific chapter last because I believe discipline and integrity are the chief values of acquiring your goals to make profound, transformative, and sustainable changes.

I'm obviously no sage of discipline. Discipline is hard because it's a full-time activity. I know there is no abiding success without absolute discipline. Discipline is leaning into resistance and taking action despite how you feel. It's the constant awareness of the need to get things to move forward.

The VOICE within us says, *"Get it done!"*

DISCIPLINE whispers, *"Do it now!"*

While INTEGRITY screams, *"Do it to the best of your abilities!"*

An immediate reward for lack of discipline is a vacation at a Hilton. A future reward of discipline is owning the vacation home. When you lack discipline, you choose today's pleasure over tomorrow's fortune.

Personally, discipline is a personal code of conduct and a commitment to high standards. But it's not just executing and getting things done – it's thinking about how you interpret who you are as an individual.

People go around labeling themselves. It's easy to go through life when people label you.

Unqualified, unattractive, average, limited, ordinary, loser, not smart enough, too old, too tall, too short, too dumb, inexperienced, unmotivated, too poor, too affluent, too ugly, too qualified, etc. If you believe the lies and the circumstances told to us, it will keep us away from our potential. Who do you believe you are?

How do you see yourself? It takes discipline to continue to vet yourself. What's holding people back is their own limited perception.

If there is anything I want you to take away, are three things:

Apply discipline to get to know who you are.

You are blessed, bright, valuable, favored, talented, creative, prosperous; you are more than enough. You are a giant, well able, confident, whole, and overcomer. You have the power to determine your destiny. Your assignment is to elevate yourself and go way beyond the perception that is holding you back.

Secondly, be brave.

As you may know, I've been a Buccaneers fan for some time. When I think about being BRAVE, I think of the teams' defensive end Pierre-Paul. Pierre-Paul sustained a serious hand injury in a fireworks accident, blowing off a significant portion of his fingers. But he didn't let that stop him from playing in the NFL. Despite being told he would never be able to play again, Pierre-Paul found the courage to work hard and accept his injury.

Pierre-Paul learned to believe in himself and go after his goals. That's courage. Rather than be discouraged with things out of his control, he trained hard and made the team. Being brave is not gifted. Being brave is a choice. We are constantly being faced with choices that put courage on the line every single day.

Bow out or keep pushing.

Give up or go all in.

Accept No or Say No Way.

I believe Pierre-Paul embraced the mindset of *"So What – Now What."* He chose Courage.

Thirdly, I hope you choose to GIVE rather than TAKE. Become a luminary to those around you and give people what life has given you.

There is nothing you can't achieve.

Keep this in mind, prioritize these lessons, and watch yourself WIN.

AFTERWORD

There is nothing you can't achieve.

My true ministry has always been trying to help people meet their goals and objectives. I believe anyone with enough discipline can excel in any career, even as a content creator.

Your journey will be an evolution— stay patient— learn to tolerate time. Enjoy the journey, keep putting one foot in front of the other, project by project, shot by shot, you'll realize you've painted a picture of success.

Producing video content is an amazing experience; it's fulfilling, exciting, and unpredictable, and I truly believe it can change and impact people's lives for the better. It's all the things that make this vocation unique and irresistible.

I hope my stuttering issue helped you get on the road to being the most consistent video producer ever. I hope the foundational factors gave you a realistic insight into what you may need to build upon. While talent is important, I hope you take away that marketing is your best friend, and hard work is the only sustainable thing. I hope you employ language as a pedestal to stand on. I wish I inspired you to make communication a pivotal part of your success.

True success, however, is multi-dimensional. Friendship, family, health, and faith are embodiment of happiness and are equally important. Simply put if I were to guide you through the key points – they would be:

- An unbreakable discipline to your craft
- Expect excellence from yourself and the team
- Recognize blessings
- Dream hard
- Take action & Be kind

At the end of the day, there is hope in the idea that we can change, that we can keep growing, learning, and trying new things. The point of always improving is the backbone of this guidebook. I wish health and blessings to you and your loved ones! Now get ready to jump in the hustle pool.

GALLERY

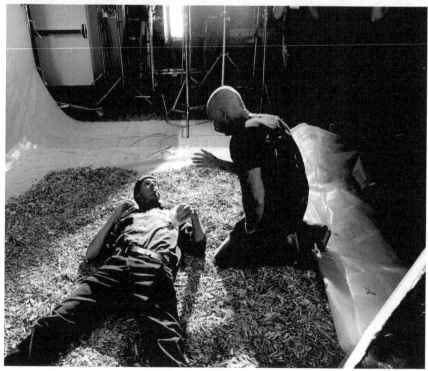

146

Producer For Hire

Made in the USA
Middletown, DE
03 April 2022

63547394R00089